What Othe

He is Looking for a Donkey, is riddled with personal experience, testimonies, stories, and biblical examples that will bring the reader to a deep and encouraging reflection. I often found myself in laughter by the way she presents the message while also recognizing the depth and importance of that message.

Marlene is an excellent communicator and writer. She has a unique gift to be very animated and well-spoken in the way she illustrates the points she is trying to get across. This book will no doubt take anyone that has a desire to go deeper in their calling, even higher in their expectation in the Lord.

I chuckled when I read this quote remembering the journey by which she lived out the challenges and crucibles of personal experience. "When people can't quite wrap their head around why the Lord would use a woman, I love to jokingly say, 'if He can use a donkey, He can use a woman,' but my favorite is, 'God uses me to confound the wise!'"

Marlene is an available and obedient servant of the Lord. My friend and fellow-servant in Christ, does confound the wise!

Doug Stringer, founder / president
Somebody Cares America
Somebody Cares International
www.SomebodyCares.Org
Houston, TX

He is Looking for a Donkey is a deep dive into the depths of the devoted Christian's struggles. It encourages the reader on how to maintain a gripping resolution of pressing through life's seasons of challenges. Finally, it brings forth the great joy and rewards set before Christians because of unwavering obedience that ultimately manifests God's Glory! A must-read for the serious Christian.

Elder Melvin Russell, Former Deputy Commissioner
Baltimore Police Department
Baltimore, MD

Marlene Yeo says, "We are all on a journey of healing. As we look into the face of Jesus and let the Holy Spirit show us our hearts and brokenness that we reflect the face of Jesus to others."

In this day of spiritual confusion and crisis of identity, how refreshing to look beyond ourselves and find others who are longing for peace and wholeness. Marlene shares her joys and struggles with such transparency and raw humanity, freely giving the keys she has discovered in the Word of God, to unlock bondages that hold humanity captive. She is truly a gift to the world through the church. As a sister in Christ, I have heard the voice of One saying, "untie her."

I celebrate this refreshing book, a warm blanket of encouragement for a donkey in the process of being tamed by His presence.

Rev Gene Heacock and **Sandy Heacock**, Founders and
Directors
Partners with Christ and *House on the Rock*
Gloucester, MA

Marlene Yeo has been my spiritual sister for over a decade. I have witnessed, firsthand, the miraculous works of God through the ministry of *Somebody Cares, New England*. To touch and see everything that God is doing in the streets throughout the New England area is inspiring.

When called upon, I went thinking I was going to minister to the people, but I was the one who received ministry. I returned home strengthened and with a deeper trust in Jesus. *He is Looking for a Donkey to Ride into Your City* captures the same inspiration as what I experienced. Marlene's work will inspire you to deepen your trust in Jesus' power that is at work within you and encourage you to trust God even when you have nothing to give. Give me ten Marlene's, and we can take any city for Jesus.

J.J. Ramirez, Evangelist
Save Our Streets Ministry
Bryan, TX

Pastor Marlene is the real deal. She leads with infectious enthusiasm, a loving heart, and zero pretension. What you see (read) is what you get. Marlene has the evident courage of her convictions through adversity, but with deep humility before the Lord, and before the needing people He has put under her care. She likens herself to the lowly donkey, carrying the love of Christ wherever He leads her especially right in her backyard. There is the calling for all of us who claim the promise, and her example has inspired me endlessly. Her passion and zeal for doing God's work jumps off the pages of this book, and onto your lap. Prepare to be challenged!

Peter Crossley, *Somebody Cares New England*
Board of Directors Treasurer
Amesbury, MA

I read the manuscript in one day! Could not put it down. The authentic and transparent presentation of how a life surrendered to the lordship of Christ can bring transformation and reformation. Reformation to individuals, family, the community of faith and city, to a region and now within reach a nation. This daughter of God shares her authentic heart to carry the ministry of Jesus to her sphere of influence and far beyond. Her life is a life well lived! Her passion and follow through to be the hands and feet of Jesus to whomever, wherever and whatever Jesus would desire. It is a just and accurate statement to say that she is a carrier of intercession and the Spirit of freedom. She is apostolically anointed and commissioned to reveal God in His goodness. She got her eyes of fire from her Daddy's (Abba) side. Her heart of love from her Savior/Shepherd and her snap finger obedience from The Holy Spirit Himself. When Jesus gives her a "YES," there ain't no telling her "NO!" She is the real deal.

This book is a must-read for everyone. Because it so lovingly kicks one in the seat of the pants to stand up and be counted, to believe that God has greatness planned for us! I am refreshed and renewed by her message! I have personally repented and relented. I heard the Spirit of God through her voice. I am more determined than ever before to invite the King of Glory to set down upon my life and do, go, and be all He would like to with and through me. Read at your own risk of being activated again and renewed for The King's purposes at this moment. Yup, that's the sound of my bray declaring, this donkey is in for the ride of his life.

A friend and a fan!

Daniel Wermuth, Lead Pastor
Joplin Family Worship Center
Joplin, MO

"The bread in your cupboard belongs to the hungry man; the coat hanging in your closet belongs to the man who needs it; the shoes rotting in your closet belong to the man who has no shoes; the money which you put into the bank belongs to the poor. You do wrong to everyone you could help but fail to help." -- Basil of Caesarea, 330-370 A.D.

The scripture tells us the early church had the same heart and spirit. You will find our God identifies himself with the poor, the broken-hearted, the outcasts, and weak in contrast to the world celebrating the powerful and wealthy. In Matthew 25, Jesus tells us He is hungry, sick, imprisoned—an outcast, and whenever or however, we serve those in need, we are serving Him personally!

I met Marlene well over twenty years ago when she visited our church for the first time, from that moment until now, I have witnessed her work tirelessly and sacrificially pouring out her life for others. Her passion is contagious for the hurting, the broken, and those often overlooked by society. It has been my joy at *Compassion Coalition Utica* to partner with Marlene's ministry on numerous occasions to assist her in outreaches she has planned in her region and beyond.

This book is an expression of Marlene's overflowing love for people. I encourage you as you read let your heart be encouraged, but most of all, let it inspire you to be a willing vessel God could flow through to bless others.

Pastor Mike Servello, Sr, Founder
Redeemer Church
Utica, NY
Founder & CEO
Compassion Coalition
Utica, NY

I meet Pastor Marlene Yeo over twenty years ago. I was impressed with her dedication to the local church and her heart for the needy. She not only had a burden from the Lord but purposed to do something about it. It is beautiful to see the Lord using her ministry to leave a legacy in so many lives.

Marlene is the founder and director of *Somebody Cares New England*, the founder, and Pastor of the *Community Christian Fellowship* of Haverhill, Ma., and the founder and director of He Cares for Me a ministry of and deliverance and healing. This book is an extension of Marlene's heart and life. It will encourage you to believe and step out in faith though you may feel like a donkey God has a plan and purpose for you. God needs each one of his children. Written out of a spirit of humility, love, and service, this book will bless you.

Rita Fedele, Cofounder
Prophetic Voice Ministries International
International Prophetic School
Prophetic Consultation Service
Global Ministers Fellowship Founder,
SWAT- Spiritual Women Apprehending Truth

It was April 2004 that I met the "Mother Teresa of New England," Pastor Marlene Yeo. Her concern and passion for the spiritual well-being of the city of Haverhill was the impetus for my exhaustive examination of the transformation movements that had occurred previously, both nationally and abroad. My research revealed God's great love for the city - his heartbeat.

"And should I not have concern for the great city of Nineveh in which there are more than a hundred and twenty thousand people who cannot tell their right hand from their left?" Jonah 4:11.

Pastor Marlene's authentic Kingdom insights detail the biblical apostolic function and the ingredients that our Holy God looks for in human vessels for us to become Presence carrier's to our cities. From one donkey to another, I salute and respect this mighty apostolic woman of God. Her book will challenge and transform the reader from an average vessel to a vessel of honor.

Apostle Rafael Najem
CCF Ministries, Inc.
Pastor *CCF Ministries*
105 Princeton Blvd.
Lowell, MA

He is looking for a Donkey is full of purpose, inspiring us to obey what God is calling us to do. As I read, it moved my spirit with great peace and new understanding, and it gave me a fuller mindset of my purpose. I highly recommend and endorse this book.

Dr. Negiel Bigpond
Two Rivers Native American Training Center
Morning Star Church of All Nations
Mounds, OK

He Is Looking
For A Donkey
To Ride into Your City

Marlene J. Yeo

Unless otherwise noted, Scripture quotes are from the NKJV Bible

The Donkey Descent into Jerusalem by Artist Martha Temple used by permission.
Author photo copyright by Diane Brown Photography

WORLD WIDE
PUBLISHING GROUP

7710-T Cherry Park Dr, Ste 224
Houston, TX 77095
(713) 766-4271

Printed in the United States of America

ISBN: 978-1-68411-871-7

Dedicated to Maureen McGee

She has had a long, challenging road and is one of the bravest women I know. She has overcome more obstacles than the average bear. Maureen is one of the rescued ones I have the joy of serving alongside in the ministry of Somebody Cares New England.

If being sent to Haverhill was just for Maureen, then it would be worth it all! Everyone who encounters Maureen can feel the love of God exude from her. It is not uncommon to see Maureen at a Sunday morning service on her face at the altar worshiping the One she loves! I have been impacted and encouraged by her love for God and her servant's heart.

I love you to life, Maureen McGee!

Contents

Introduction

"'If it had not been the Lord who was on our side,'"
Let Israel now say..."
Psalm 124:1

The purpose of this book is to give glory to God for the miraculous power of His love. I hope to provide both natural and spiritual insight to provide guidance and encouragement along your personal and community journey of transformation.

If I were to have a disclaimer, it would read: I was just like that donkey tied to a tree. Jesus sent His disciples to unloose me and bring me to Him. He said to them, "If anyone says anything, you shall say, 'The Lord needs her,' and immediately she went."

I am just a small part of the larger church body who have answered the call to pray and serve my city and nation. I know of no formula or manual that will guarantee the transformation of a community or country. But when we obey biblical principles with a heart of humility, it creates an atmosphere of faith, peace, and love, which attracts His presence. It creates an opening for His presence where He finds a resting place from which He will work in miraculous ways.

If it had not been for the Lord on my side and sending His faithful ministers to unloose me, I would not be on the journey of transformation today. Only God knows where I would be. God gave me Kingdom relationships that walk with me even when I didn't think I could keep on keeping on. They have pastored my soul. Like a good shepherd, they wiped my crusted eyes, sheared my heavy wool, anointed me with oil to keep away the flies and cleaned my hooves. They are those on the same journey of transformation with me.

When wounded in my Father's house, they corrected me when I spoke fearful, faithless words. They demonstrated compassion when I needed it most. They trained, instructed, and guided me with wisdom.

Without their Christ-like love and dedicated commitment to my well-being and the call on my life, I would not be where I am today. Because they stood up for me and stood in the gap for me might be one of the reasons why, when watching the movie, "Sing," with my grandkids, I enthusiastically get into the song, "Still Standing."

> "Don't you know I'm still standing, better than I ever did
>
> Looking like a true survivor, feeling like a little kid
>
> I'm still standing after all this time, yeah, yeah yeah."

Yeah, still standing, thanks to my Redeemer! Because of His mercy and His ministers, I am not only standing but by His grace, running the race at a steady pace. When we look at the ten commandments and the cross, they are both vertical and horizontal, representing our relationship with both God and man. We are in Christ and interconnected with each other for Kingdom purpose. Before I mention them, I want to thank God for my husband. Harry Yeo, thank you for encouraging me to answer the call, covering, praying, and providing for me in so many ways.

All my beautiful friends are seasoned, mature ministers who function in the fivefold ministry gifts. They are all church planters, apostles, prophets, evangelists, pastors, and teachers. Their names, according to the timeline, God graced me with their friendship. Beginning with the first in 1994, Dan Wermuth II was instrumental in connecting me with Chad Waller. Through Stephen and Rita Fedele, I met Pastor Michael Servello Jr. and Pastor Mike Servello Sr. Dr. Doug Stringer introduced me to Matt Stevens and J.J. Ramirez, and last but not least, in 2004, my pastor, Apostle Rafael Najem.

Thank you! Thank you for being true shepherds under the Great Shepherd. The Lord has used you to impact not only me but thousands of lives and ministries. You are strong, yet in your strength, you are gentle. Each one's heart is to see His Kingdom come and His will be done, on earth, in His church (and in me) as it is in heaven. Thank you for mentoring me in the ministry and for caring for my soul. May you reap one hundredfold for the loving kindness you have shown me throughout the years and for loving me to life. May the Lord reward you all for serving Him well! *Assuredly, I say to you, inasmuch as you did it to one of the least of these My brethren, you did it to Me.* (Matthew 25:40)

Matthew 21 and Zachariah 9 has inspired the title of this book. It is no coincidence while in His mother's womb, they rode into Bethlehem on a donkey. The final days of His ministry, Jesus rode a donkey into Jerusalem to die on a cross for humanity. Old Testament Scripture told us He was coming on a donkey, which was fulfilled in Matthew 21.

> *Rejoice greatly, O daughter of Zion! Shout, O daughter of Jerusalem! Behold, your King is coming to you; He is just and having salvation, lowly and riding on a donkey, a colt, the foal of a donkey.* (Zechariah 9:9)

> *Jesus, saying to them, "Go into the village opposite you, and immediately you will find a donkey tied, and a colt with her. Loose them and bring them to Me. And if anyone says anything to you, you shall say, 'The Lord has need of them,' and immediately he will send them." All this was done that it might be fulfilled which was spoken by the prophet, saying: 'Tell the daughter of Zion, 'Behold, your King is coming to you, Lowly, and sitting on a donkey, A colt, the foal of a donkey.' So the disciples went and did as Jesus commanded them. They brought the donkey and the colt, laid their clothes on them, and set Him on them."* (Matt 21:2-7)

This book is a user-friendly source of encouragement for those who want to be a part of something bigger than themselves, for those who want to be a part of God's redemptive plan for their family, church, city, and nation. And for those ruined with His heart of love for the ones who don't yet know Him.

It's for ordinary people, like me, who make themselves available as a donkey that Jesus can ride into our Jerusalem. Our

Jerusalem is the location where you have a realm of influence and authority. God has a plan, a purpose, and a destiny for every person, family, city, and nation. He invites us to be a part of the journey of restoration and transformation. In Isaiah 58:12 we read, *Those from among you shall build the old waste places; You shall raise the foundations of many generations; And you shall be called the Repairer of the Breach, The Restorer of Streets to Dwell In.*

From Genesis to Revelation, Scripture reveals God's plan for the ones He created to be intimately acquainted with Him, to walk in His power and authority, to tend His garden, and rule with Him over cities and nations. He even promises to give us the power to do so. Acts 1:8 says, *"But you shall receive power when the Holy Spirit has come upon you; and you shall be witnesses to Me in Jerusalem, and in all Judea and Samaria, and to the end of the earth."*

His Word makes known His desire for the church to partner with Him to love the world beginning in our own Jerusalem. Most often, the city God assigned to you is the city you live in or may end up living in.

In our day and age, there are very few who attend a local church in the same city they live in. It is astounding how many believers live in one town and yet attend church in another city or even state. The church is the heartbeat of the community. When believers live in one location attending church in another city or state, they are not living out the mandate *"first in their Jerusalem."* Therefore, you cannot vote, as you have no legal right to speak into the life of the city you attend church.

How is it that we have become so disconnected, so disinterested, so disillusioned to think it doesn't matter? Now, I am not judging commuters; I get why we do it. For 27 years, I commuted across town, city, and state lines. I am not finding fault with people who commute. The people are not the issue, what the local church teaches and how it functions has created a problem.

At a statewide pastors' conference called *Issachar Training*, sponsored by the *American Renewal Project*, I met two pastors who were sitting at my table. Both lived in my city and pastored churches 40-50 minutes from Haverhill. The speaker in one session had us interact with each other at the table to answer the following questions:

- Who are the officials that serve the community, that you pastor?

- How often does your church gather and pray for the leaders of the city?

- How is your church serving the people in the city?

- How many in your congregation are registered to vote?

- How many active voters are involved in the life of the community?

- How is your church reaching the people within the block your church is located?

Throughout the Bible, we see that the church, God's people, are called to be the salt and the light of a city.

You are the salt of the earth; but if the salt loses its flavor, how shall it be seasoned? It is then good for nothing but to be thrown out and trampled underfoot by men. "You are the light of the world. A city that is set on a hill cannot be hidden. Nor do they *light a lamp and put it under a basket, but on a lampstand, and it gives light to all who are in the house. Let your light so shine before men, that they may see your good works and glorify your Father in heaven. (*Matthew 5: 13-16*)*

I love that it was *just a concerned citizen* that penned the book of Nehemiah; he was not a priest or a government official; he was a servant of the king. He saw the condition of the city of Jerusalem and the people of God. His heart broke, he sat down, wept and repented on behalf of a nation. He gave himself to the purposes of God and was used to change a nation. The Bible is full of stories about ordinary people (donkeys) that God used to do the impossible.

God's heart breaks over the state of the church and the ruin of cities. For the suffering children, the isolated elderly, and those trapped in a lifestyle of sin. We are often too busy with our own lives to notice, care, or change the way we do things to make room in our lives to reach out and serve the people that live in our zip code while the church has its sound bite Sunday morning service.

Multitudes of churches are moving out of the so-called "danger zone" of the inner city into the suburbs. I do hope it is not because they are more concerned with paying bills and salaries. Country folks need Jesus just as much as the urban, low-income population because our Father's heart is concerned for both. I am reminded of Reverend Dave Wilkerson, founder of *Teen Challenge*, moving into the heart of an unsafe, poverty-stricken city.

God cares for the babies who wear the same diaper all day long, whose playpen is the pavement, for the children and youth left to fend for themselves in the middle of bullying, violence, and addictions. There are generations of abuse and poverty in families, primarily due to fathers who walked out on their children to sire more babies down the street. I have heard this generation referred to as "Kodak Kids," which describes them best, overexposed and underdeveloped. Overexposed to perversion, addictions, and pain and underdeveloped to succeed in life. I feel God's heart of compassion for the elderly who sit alone without proper nutrition or care, day after day, staring out the window of their subsidized housing.

He is looking for those who are willing to give themselves to prayer and the work of compassion like Count Zinzendorf, Mother Theresa, Heidi Baker, John Elliot, Jackie Pullinger, and Doug Stringer to name a few. He is looking for those who have given themselves to be His warrior bride, who are the lovers of humanity and will fight for social justice. We, the army of the Living God, are called out of the darkness and sent out to carry the light of His presence everywhere we go.

"May the Lamb receive the reward of His suffering!"

Count Zinzendorf.

Chapter One

A Donkey for a King?

I chose the title for this book for two reasons; one due to the characteristics of the donkey and two, which is the primary reason, because of Old Testament prophecy and New Testament Scriptures regarding the Messiah.

A donkey was the means through which Father God chose to carry His Son Jesus into His destiny. The first donkey carried Christ while in His mother's womb to His place of birth, Bethlehem. The second donkey to Jerusalem for His death, burial, and resurrection, so *we could be born* into the Kingdom of God!

> *.... then Jesus sent two disciples, 2 saying to them, "Go into the village opposite you, and immediately you will find a donkey tied and a colt with her. Loose them and bring them to Me. 3 And if anyone says anything to you, you shall say, 'The Lord has need of them,' and immediately he will send them." 4 All this was done that it might be fulfilled which was spoken by the prophet, saying: 5 "Tell the daughter of Zion, 'Behold, your King is coming to you, lowly, and sitting on a donkey, a colt, the foal of a donkey.'*
> (Matthew 21:1-5)

Matthew 21:5 is a direct quote from Zachariah 9:9. The mention of a donkey fits the description of the coming King as "righteous, having salvation and gentle." In biblical times the royal world leaders rode horses if they were riding into war, but donkeys if they came in peace. Rather than riding to conquer, this King Jesus would enter Jerusalem in peace. Born of a virgin, as this baby King came to die for the sins of the world, He was lowly and meek.

The return of the soon coming King will be riding a white horse. He will come declaring war against His enemies.

> *Then I saw heaven opened, and behold, a white horse! The one sitting on it is called Faithful and True, and in righteousness, he judges and makes war. His eyes are like a flame of fire, and on his head are many diadems, and he has a name written that no one knows but himself. He is clothed in a robe dipped in blood, and the name by which he is called is The Word of God. And the armies of heaven, arrayed in fine linen, white and pure, were following him on white horses. From his mouth comes a sharp sword with which to strike down the nations, and he will rule them with a rod of iron. He will tread the winepress of the fury of the wrath of God the Almighty... (Rev 19:11-16)*

More on this soon returning King in the last chapter of this book. The Donkey is known as a beast of burden, "a lumpa" (Boston overtone). Donkeys are domesticated animals trained to perform tasks. They survive in drought conditions, are hard workers, and able to carry or pull heavy loads. The donkey has a unique marking on its back in the shape of a cross. As legend would have it, God placed the mark of the cross on the donkey's back as a prophetic sign that the beast of burden would carry, not only the mother of Jesus to His prophetic place of birth, but also the Son of God to the prophetic place of death.

In Numbers 22, it was a donkey that God used to save Balaam's life. This story reveals the heart of God for humanity. We, like Balaam, are perverse, rebellious, and offensive to the Spirit of God. We deserve punishment for our sins, calling judgment upon ourselves, yet the heart of the Father uses a beast of burden to intercept our judgment. Because a donkey's nature is known as stubborn, obstinate, stupid or lacking common sense, a person with those characteristics is referred to as "dumb - - -." Technically I could use the King James Bible version name for a donkey here, but I will refrain, you get the point.

I can relate to the donkey in Matthew 21:1-3: *...you will find a donkey tied, and a colt with her. Loose them and bring them to Me. 3 And if anyone says anything to you, you shall say, 'The Lord has need of them,'* The Lord rescued me from bondage, and drew me to Himself. If anyone asks, He will answer, "I chose her to carry My presence into this city."

This book is a testimony of my calling as an intercessor. I am a prayer; compassion missionary sent out by the Lord to Haverhill, Massachusetts.

My assignment is to pray for and love the people and to bless the city. When people can't quite wrap their heads around why the Lord would use a woman, I like to jokingly say, "If He can use a donkey, He can use a woman," my favorite answer is, "God uses me to confound the wise!" I Corinthians 1:27 says, *But God has chosen the foolish things of the world to put to shame the wise, and God has chosen the weak things of the world to put to shame the things which are mighty.*

That's what the Sovereign Lord does. He chooses the ones that don't appear to be wise to reveal His glory through the foolish and the base. I like the dictionary definition of base used in the context of "building, the distinctively treated lowermost". And there it is, He rescues the "lowermost" and carries them into His "uttermost." Only one of the billion reasons I love Him so!

It is hard to explain the most glorious feeling I get when the Holy Spirit connects the history of a person, place, or thing to present-day events and brings the spiritual significance into focus for the future. To my utter amazement, the archaic dictionary definition for glorious is, *"blissfully drunk"*! So I guess it would be ok, by dictionary definition, to say, I get *blissfully drunk*, in the Spirit (that is), when I get to pray by divine revelation into the intended design and purpose of God.

As we learn of what He has done in the past, it is often an indicator of what He wants us to partner with Him to pray in the present and what He will manifest in the future. I have documented many testimonies of how God has advanced His Kingdom using this foolish donkey to do so.

The Lord used my friend Susan as one of many confirmations for the title, "He is Looking for a Donkey to ride into your city." It is yet, another testimony of how over the top awesome the Lord is. My friend Karen Chitty-Boe, who lives in Texas, graduated from Zion (renamed Northpoint) Bible College with Pastor Susan Herron Moniz in 1978. At the time I met Susan, she and her husband George pastored New Hope Assembly of God Church in Tonopah, Nevada.

Karen has a unique and beautiful gift from the Lord to network strategic relationships for Kingdom purposes. She and Susan flew to Haverhill specifically for Susan to connect with me. Karen felt the Lord was up to something good. We spent three days together, sharing what God was doing in our lives. We had the sense of the time spent together as part of His destiny for us all.

Susan shared about pastoring, using her words, in a Podunk town, in Tonopah, Nevada. She encouraged me to research for myself about Tonopah. I did just that and was blown away by what I discovered.

I knew God was relating the natural to the spiritual and speaking to me about intercession. The following information is extrapolated and paraphrased from the Tonopah history website, dictionary, Wikipedia, and the Bible.

Tonopah Springs, later the site of one of the richest booms in the West, was an Indian campground for many years. Jim Butler discovered silver ore in Tonopah Springs in the spring of 1900, he and his wife Belle filed claims for eight mines. The largest, called Mizpah, produced the most silver of all. It continued producing long after the other mines tapped out. 'Mizpah' is Hebrew for *watchtower*, also meaning an emotional bond and agreement between two people who are separated by long distances. Several stories exist as to how Butler discovered the ore. One version is that Butler's donkey wandered off, and when Butler later found the ornery critter, he noticed an outcropping laced with silver.

Characteristics of a donkey are associated with the very poor, with those living at or below the poverty level. Donkeys have a reputation for stubbornness, but this is due to their highly developed sense of self-preservation. They adapt to desert conditions well. Likely based on a stronger prey instinct and a weaker connection with humans, it is considerably more difficult to force or frighten a donkey into doing something it perceives to be dangerous, for whatever reason. Once a person has earned their confidence, donkeys can be willing and companionable partners, very dependable and hard-working.

Although formal studies of their behavior and cognition are somewhat limited, donkeys appear to be quite intelligent, cautious, friendly, playful, and eager to learn. They are bred as work animals, used for agricultural purposes, and transport as beasts of burden. In contrast, horses are represented in the context of war, ridden by cavalry or pulling chariots.

In the Jewish religion, the donkey is considered the ultimate impure animal. However, it is the only unclean animal that falls under the mitzvah (commandment) of firstborn consecration that also applies to humans and pure animals.

The Lord is looking for burden bearers who are not afraid of hard work under challenging conditions. Intercessors likened to a "beast of burden" are called to a fasted lifestyle. Although it includes seasons of fasting food, it is more about choosing a lifestyle of abstaining from what is permissible for something better.

For instance, I had the right to spend my early mornings relaxing in my pajamas.

But instead, every Monday through Friday for three years, I abstained from what I had a right to do and chose early morning prayer for the city with other intercessors. Disciples of Christ live a fasted lifestyle of obedience as we care for one another. When we do so, the Lord will use us to rebuild and restore cities making the community livable again. Isaiah 58:1-12, MSG reads,

> "Shout! A full-throated shout! Hold nothing back—a trumpet-blast shout! Tell my people what's wrong with their lives, face my family Jacob with their sins!
>
> They're busy, busy, busy at worship, and love studying all about me. To all appearances, they're a nation of right-living people— law-abiding, God-honoring. They ask me, 'What's the right thing to do?' and love having me on their side. But they also complain, 'Why do we fast and you don't look our way? Why do we humble ourselves and you don't even notice?'
>
> "Well, here's why: "The bottom line on your 'fast days' is profit. You drive your employees much too hard. You fast, but at the

same time, you bicker and fight. You fast, but you swing a mean fist. The kind of fasting you do won't get your prayers off the ground. Do you think this is the kind of fast day I'm after a day to show off humility? To put on a pious long face and parade around solemnly in black? Do you call that fasting, a fast day that I, God, would like?

"This is the kind of fast day I'm after: to break the chains of injustice, get rid of exploitation in the workplace, free the oppressed, cancel debts.

What I'm interested in seeing you do is sharing your food with the hungry, inviting the homeless poor into your homes, putting clothes on the shivering ill-clad, being available to your own families Do this and the lights will turn on, and your lives will turn around at once. Your righteousness will pave your way. The God of glory will secure your passage. Then when you pray, God will answer. You will call out for help, and I'll say, 'Here I am.' A Full Life in the Emptiest of Places.

"If you get rid of unfair practices quit blaming victims, quit gossiping about other people's sins, If you are generous with the hungry and start giving yourselves to the down-and-out, Your lives will begin to glow in the darkness, your shadowed lives will be bathed in sunlight. I will always show you where to go. I'll give you a full life in the emptiest of places— firm muscles, strong bones, You'll be like a well-watered garden, a gurgling spring that never runs dry. You'll use the old rubble of past lives to build a new, rebuild the foundations from out of your past. You'll be known as those who can fix anything, restore old ruins, rebuild and renovate, make the community livable again."

When His Word, His name, and the power of His blood is declared over cities, strongholds are displaced. He will establish a beachhead of prayer in every city that He finds willing vessels. Come what may and come it did! Hell is not happy when we stand in the gap for souls, cities, and nations. The spiritual entity that we pray to be displaced and striped of its authority, is the same entity that counter-attacks trying to gain strongholds over the life, health, finances, and family of the intercessor. But as the battle rages, we are not ignorant of the devil's devices so, we stand on the Word of the Lord and declare with confidence Isaiah 54:17, *No weapon formed against you shall prosper, and every tongue which rises against you in judgment You shall condemn. This is the heritage of the servants of the Lord, and their righteousness is from Me," Says the Lord.*

As we decree, the enemy is defeated, and we will not be moved. 1 Corinthians 15:55-58 says,

"O Death, where is your sting. O Hades, where is your victory?" 56 The sting of death is sin, and the strength of sin is the law. 57 But thanks be to God, who gives us the victory through our Lord Jesus Christ 58 Therefore, my beloved brethren, be steadfast, immovable, always abounding in the work of the Lord, knowing that your labor is not in vain in the Lord."

It was a relief to my soul to hear the prophetic word of the Lord one Saturday night while attending service at *Redeemer Church* in Utica, NY. Prophet Stephen Fedele spoke these words over me, "You haven't done this on purpose, but you have made a lot of people mad, I hear them saying, 'Is she still here? Isn't she gone already?' They tried to discourage you and remove you, but you stayed, and God has sustained and kept you." God is so kind as to confirm the words spoken by His prophets.

Several months after receiving this prophetic word, I was running an errand for my husband at the Firefighters Credit Union. I ran into a retired Lieutenant, I knew. We had attended the same high school. I had all I could do not to let my jaw hang down to the floor when he boldly belted out, "Marlene Yeo, the city of Haverhill threw everything they had against you to try to get you out of that city block, but you didn't back down."

If that wasn't confirmation enough, during the early years when the Lord sent me to Haverhill as a watchman intercessor for the city, He gave us many specific assignments to pray. I invited my friend Linda Clark to be a part of several of our prayer assignments. I will share more in other chapters of this book.

Linda is an apostolic leader that has served the New England Region as the Apostolic Regional Coordinator for both USRPN (US regional Prayer Network), HAPN (Heartland Apostolic Prayer Network), the USRPN headed by Dr. Cindy Jacobs and the HAPN, Dr. John Benefiel. She was commissioned as an apostle by Apostle Negiel Bigpond during a historic "Sound of Arising Gathering" in Springfield MA on November 29, 2011.

Linda was led by the Lord to go on assignment in England, and there she met Deborah who was an intercessor in England involved with the same prayer assignment as Linda. Deborah received a clear directive from the Lord and said to Linda, "Do you know of a city called Haverhill?" Deborah went on to say, "The Lord spoke to me that I am to go to the States to pray in Washington DC, New York City, Boston, and Haverhill," and

Deborah did just that! She came to pray and prophesy the word of the Lord. God used her to confirm my assignment. Without knowing anything about Haverhill's history, she confirmed God's heart and destiny for my city.

Everything Deborah said was spot on! It was one of those holy moments of divine appointment. The words God gave her to speak were like an anchor in my soul. She was one of many prophets that God used to solidify the call on my life and confirm the destiny of Haverhill. I knew that I knew, that no weapon formed against me would or could prosper. The Lord was my defense and strong tower!

It is interesting to note that my name in Hebrew means "*a strong tower*" where the righteous run and are safe. The origin of the name is German. It was created by combining two names Maria and Magdalene (Mar-lene), in homage to Mary Magdalene from the New Testament, who was from Magdala, a village on the Sea of Galilee. Magdala comes from a Hebrew word meaning "*tower*," in Aramaic, meaning "*elevated, high place*." Mary was the closest female disciple of Jesus, and one of the two women that Jesus Himself appeared and the one the angel said, "*go and tell the brothers He has risen as He said!*"

I love the scene in the Passion of the Christ, where Mary Magdalene is prostrate on the ground, about to be stoned by her accusers. She reaches out to touch the feet of Jesus, and He reaches out to raise her, elevate her, to the highest place of His love, forgiving her sin, giving her dignity and worth in the sight of her accusers. Mary, the woman caught in adultery and was now, Mary, the disciple of Christ.

Luke 8:2-3 mentions Mary as one of the women who traveled with Jesus and supported his ministry. She was a witness to the crucifixion, death, and resurrection of Jesus, and the first to testify of Jesus' resurrection to the apostles. Thus the reason, known in many Christian traditions, as the "apostle to the apostles." In many Christian writings, Mary is known as Jesus' closest disciple as Luke 7:47 states whoever is forgiven much, loves much!

The meaning of a name has significance. Haverhill is the English name the settlers gave our city. As history tells the story, the land was occupied, established and named by the Native Americans as Pentucket, which means "place of the long and winding river." I love the verse in Ezekiel that speaks of the river. Ezekiel 47:9 *And it shall be that every living thing that moves, wherever the rivers go, will live. There will be a very great multitude of fish because these waters go there; for they will be healed, and everything will live wherever the river goes.*

It is interesting to note that over the years, Haverhill has cleaned up the Merrimack River, which was once polluted by industry. Since the river restoration, one of the most ancient fish, the Sturgeon, has migrated from Maine to Haverhill. There has yet to be any reason determined for this phenomenon. I believe it is a prophetic sign of revival.

In 1642 'Pentucket' was renamed Haverhill, which is two words: haver, and hill. Webster's definition of both terms translates "possessor of the hill." The Marlene Yeo spin on it reads, Jesus is "King of the Hill." God ministered to me about being a watchman from Psalm 127:1, *"Unless the Lord builds the house, they labor in vain who build it; Unless the Lord guards the city, the watchman stays awake in vain."*

The watchmen are not the ones who guard the city; the Lord is. The watchmen are just the bearer of burden and donkeys of intercession who make themselves available to pray as the Lord leads. He raises us up, as it were, on wings like eagles. It is from that place, and only that place, that we exercise true spiritual authority as we are seated with Him in the high tower of His presence through prayer.

Margret Foley is a researcher that God uses to equip intercessors with insight from history to pray God's will and destiny on sight. One day as we were on one of our prayer adventures, we felt impressed to go to the highest place in the city. We felt directed by the Holy Spirit to bind the prince of the air, to be stripped of authority, and to declare the message of the cross of Christ heard over Haverhill.

Peg had learned from research there were radio towers on one of the highest hills in Haverhill. The road on our map that appeared to lead us there was named Lovers Lane! Here we were, little donkeys, compelled by His love to pray for our city and the road that led to the high place is named Lovers Lane. Although lover's lane, had a bad connotation, to the pure all things are pure. We were so intent on seeing the redemptive qualities that we were innocent, or maybe a better word is naive.

We drove as far as we could on the dead-end road, got out, locked the car, and started the ascent to the high place, all happy with ourselves, giggling like little kids at the irony of it all. After arriving at the top of the hill, we could see for miles as we looked

21

over Haverhill, the beautiful city of God. Remember, haver means one who possesses a hill or high place. Here we were feeling exhilarated that we were declaring "Christ the King" as Possessor of the Hill! We were just about to start praying when suddenly, this 4x4 comes ramming up the hill and out jumps this rather rugged lady yelling, "Don't you know this is private property!"

We were all amazed and rather dumbfounded as I slowly answered, "Ah, well, no, actually we never saw a sign stating it was private. We are sorry, no harm intended." She proceeded to tell us we could find access to this same location from another road, named Elijah Street. We apologized again and quietly trotted down the hill to our car. Once inside we started to laugh hysterically, what? How did we miss Elijah Street on our map? This adventure was just one of our joyous, memorable moments etched in our hearts forever.

Sure enough, there we were at the top of Elijah Street, reminded of the biblical record of Elijah confronting the prophets of Baal. Here we were, just little ladies (donkeys), obedient intercessors standing in the gap, confronting the prince of the power of the air, declaring the message of the cross to be preached through the airwaves of our beloved city!

Very shortly after, a Christian radio station out of Maine was considering Haverhill as the perfect place for one of their radio towers. God used "Inside Out Soul Festival" founder Dan Russell to contact me, asking if Somebody Cares New England would host a regional gathering to assess the interest of

Merrimack Valley churches in partnering with the radio station. Today we have K-Love radio in the valley, praise the Lord!

In addition to that exciting happening, it wasn't long afterward I was invited by the CEO of the Haverhill Community TV to produce the Somebody Cares New England TV show, a local cable station, which we aired for over seven years. The guests I invited were my relationships that God had connected me with over many years.

My guests ranged from former addicts and homeless that God rescued, secular business owners, and agency directors that were impacted by Somebody Cares, as well as intercessors and pastors from across New England and the USA. One of my friends, who traveled from the uttermost part of the world, is an international minister and author, Pastor Suliasi Kurulo. You can read about his life and ministry in his book "The Ends of the Earth." Pastor Suliasi is the founder of Christian Mission Fellowship, which has trained hundreds of evangelists and missionaries and planted more than 6,000 churches in more than 100 nations, mostly among formerly unreached people.

Suli, as called by his friends, pastors the world's largest church in the southern hemisphere, as well as founder and director of Somebody Cares Fiji. His testimony of God transforming Fiji is documented on the transformation video, "Let the Seas Resound," produced by George Otis and the Sentinel Group. Suli is one of the intercessors God used for the revival in Fuji. God has used him to build a hospital, Bible college, and Christian school. I first met this man at the Somebody Cares Summit in Houston, Texas. After I spoke in one of the sessions, he said to me, "I only come to the United States once a year, this year, I am coming to your city." I responded with unbelief, "Oh, we are just a small city, and I pastor a small church with a small budget."

I couldn't imagine how we could afford to have him come. I felt the gentle Holy Spirit correction by his response, "I am not coming to your city because of what you do or don't have. I am coming because I sense the DNA of city transformation, and I am coming because of what God is doing."

I remember when I watched the first Transformation video in 1999, how I prayed then and still pray today, "Lord, transform me, my family, my church, my city, and my nation. I want to be a part of what You are doing in the nations of the world, Lord."

Now, here I was hosting Reverend Suliasi in my home and church. Isn't that just like the Lord to send this man of God from the uttermost, Fuji, to Haverhill, Massachusetts, to confirm my calling and the Lord's plan for the transformation of my city? Every time I think about it, I am overwhelmed that I get to be a part of His great plan for this little city that I liken to little Bethlehem. No one would ever suspect the Lord is working such great things in such a lowly city.

As an intercessor, we must be willing to be the lowly, humble donkey! Our prayers in the spiritual realm will take us to places in the natural as we often find ourselves to be the very ones God uses to answer the prayers we prayed, go figure! Back to my divine appointment at the Fire Fighters Credit Union, it was a God moment for me. I had a greater revelation that the fear of man was no longer my master. I knew that God had opened the doors and planted us strategically on a city block, and nobody, whether in the natural or spiritual, was going to move me from that appointed place.

One means of rendering the powers of darkness inoperable is by coming in the opposite spirit. We displace poverty through generosity, fear through faith in action, hate through love, violence through kindness, and apathy through dedicated, sacrificial commitment. Scripture instructs when the enemy is displaced; we are to fill the house with Christ's kingdom, power, love, and authority.

To be a vessel, the Lord can use to pull down strongholds; one must know their position as His beloved. We must be confident in His love for us, or we waver in the opinions of man. In time the Holy Spirit will approve, defend, and vindicate us in the eyes of the people that He has called us to serve and lead, as He did for Aaron.

Not only did Aaron's rod bud, but it also produced flowers and almonds! (Numbers 17:8)

In the normal process of creating fruit first, a bud appears, and then it turns into a blossom. Next, the flower falls off, and then the fruit emerges. However, according to the Sages, Aaron's staff went beyond the natural process. Miraculously, Aaron's staff didn't just bear fruit; it also maintained the buds and blossoms that preceded the fruit. God wants us to know that there is great value not only in the fruit but also in the process.

The fruit is the end-product, the result of tilling the land, sowing, watering, and harvesting. Typically, we judge our success by results, the fruit of our labor. Yet, there is value in the process too. The buds and blossoms represent the process that goes into the act of creating something. The presence of all three on Aaron's branch teaches us that the journey of life is as important as the change it produces inside us, as well as is our destination.

Where are you on your journey? If you are like me, you have not yet seen the fulfillment of what the Lord has promised you. Sometimes it can be frustrating to look back knowing how far you have come yet feel so far from your destination. It is a beautiful thing to realize and accept that in the middle of the process, we are in the center of God's will, even before we see the fruit for our labor.

Who you are right now has value. I have learned to appreciate each stage in the journey of life and my place on the spiritual path. I pray that God gives you peace and strength to continue growing forward in your transformation as a vessel for others to be transformed by the power of His love.

I was invited by my friend Pastor Chad to a conference in Michigan. At the end of one of the services, I answered the altar call. Little did I know I was about to experience a holy happening.

I was at the far left of the altar. The entire front area of the church crowded with all the people who responded. As I stood there with my eyes closed, something supernatural happened. Suddenly, this man to the far right side of the altar began wailing with groans such as I never heard before. Simultaneously I lamented with the same depth of cries with the exact length of time that he did. I have no idea how long it lasted, but after some time, things began to calm down. After everyone had left, I looked down the other side to see a young black man.

I had experienced a level of intercession that was beyond my understanding. To put words to my experience is a challenge. The Scripture that best describes what happened to me is Romans 8:26-27, *Likewise the Spirit also helps in our weaknesses. For we do not know what we should pray for as we ought, but the Spirit Himself makes intercession for us with groanings which cannot be uttered. 27 Now He who searches the hearts knows what the mind of the Spirit is because He makes intercession for the saints according to the will of God.*

Following the service, everyone went back to the Wallers for lunch. I was so emotional; there was no way I could go. I asked to stay behind in Chad's office. He hesitated with concern for my well-being, but I convinced him to let me stay. I spent the next hour seeking the Lord about what just happened. The Holy Spirit reminded me that I had made myself available for Him to use me; however, He chose. I realized then I was called to intercede for the broken-hearted, those wounded by injustice, the oppressed, and those in need of healing and restoration.

What I experienced that day is what the Bible describes as prophetic intercession. It would not be the last time I would have the humbling privilege to intercede for those who have suffered a racial injustice. Later, as an intercessor, God allowed me to feel the bitter root judgments black Americans feel against white people because of racial injustice. I have prayed many times since then that our Father will forgive us and heal, restore, and vindicate those who have been sinned against by white men through the evils of prejudice and injustice. Jeremiah 27:18a says, *But if they are prophets, and if the word of the Lord is with them, let them now make intercession to the Lord of hosts.*

Will you give yourself to intercede on behalf of the Lord of Hosts? Will you give yourself to be a carrier of His presence into your Jerusalem?

Chapter Two

It Isn't Real Until it is Written

An introduction lets you know who the speaker or author is. The first four words of the Bible introduces the author, none other than, the Lord God Almighty (creator, originator, designer) of heaven and earth. In Genesis 1:1, we read: *In the beginning God...* He who spoke the Word instructed holy men to write what He spoke.

The entire first chapter of Genesis is full of, "Then God said..." What would life be like if the Lord did not instruct holy men to write His spoken words? We would be carried away by false doctrine. The Bible teaches us to obey those in authority, who speak the Word of God to us and whose conduct is in alignment with sound doctrine.

"It isn't real until it's written," is a quote from one of my most treasured wise mentors, Dr. Doug Stringer. Doug is the founder and president of *Somebody Cares America/International* and Pastor of *Turning Point Ministries*, based in Houston, Texas. I remember Doug saying, "If God had only spoken His Word and never told Moses to document what He spoke, we would not have the first five books of the Bible."

The Lord is involved in everyday life of ordinary people. I love the divine romance between God and His beloved, the church. We respond by opening the door of our heart and surrendering the seat of our will to His Lordship. He establishes His Kingdom at the epicenter of our being as we crown Him King, Master, and Ruler of our life.

As we abide (remain) in Him and He abides (remains) in us, we are matured as sons and daughters to reflect His nature here on the earth. It is the Holy Spirit breathed Word that renews, heals, and matures the spirit man. He takes our sin, shame, and sorrow, in exchange He gives us forgiveness, peace, and joy. I call it the divine exchange, my humanity for His divinity. What an amazing Father that He so lavishly crowns us with such loving kindness!

John 15:1 reads, *These things I have spoken to you, that My joy may remain in you, and that your joy may be full.* The Lord desires for us to know the fullness of joy. It starts by having a hearing ear to hear what He is speaking. We need to stand, watch and see, listen, and write it, that we may run with the instruction given. Because Lord knows, what will follow after we see and hear, then comes the test. The Word of the Lord will be tried and tested in our own heart before it comes to pass.

During the test period, when the Teacher is silent, as every teacher is quiet during the test, we are encouraged by what was written. We fight the good fight with the sword of His Word in the dark narrow passageway into the promises of God. Habakkuk 2:1-4 says,

I will stand my watch and set myself on the rampart, and watch to see what He will say to me, and what I will answer when I am corrected. 2 Then the Lord answered me and said: "Write the vision and make it plain on tablets, that he may run who reads it. 3 For the vision is yet for an appointed time, but at the end, it will speak, and it will not lie. Though it tarries, wait for it; Because it will surely come, It will not tarry. 4 "Behold the proud, His soul is not upright in him; But the just shall live by his faith."

I have been to Jerusalem and seen with my eyes the watchmen on the wall. A rampart is the surrounding embankment of a fort, often including any walls that are built on the bank. It is a raised area that elevates one to see a great distance, a protective barrier, a broad embankment raised as a fortification.

As we are positioned on the wall of intercession, seeking the Lord to speak, it is none other than the Spirit of prophecy that gives testimony to the word as stated in Revelation 19:10 *For the testimony of Jesus is the Spirit of prophecy.* May I remind us all, that what is recorded in the New Testament of what Jesus had spoken was by the Spirit. Most of which had not been previously written; it was the spoken Word. It was much later that what He spoke was written down and recorded in the Bible.

31

The religious of Jesus' day did not receive the Words He spoke. The same is true in our day. The religious still do not believe or accept the words spoken by the Spirit of prophecy. It is a fearful thing to think we can have the written Word, as did the Pharisees, yet deny that the Holy Spirit still speaks today. I can almost hear the uproar of the religious on that day as Jesus spoke in John 13:34-35, *"A new commandment I give to you, that you love one another; as I have loved you, that you also love one another. 35 By this, all will know that you are My disciples if you have love for one another."*

"What? A new commandment? We are Abraham's descendants; we have the Torah given through Moses! What authority do you have to claim you have seen the Father and speak on His behalf a new commandment?"

Jesus said, "As the Father loved Me, I also have loved you; abide in My love. 10 If you keep My commandments, you will abide in My love, just as I have kept My Father's commandments and abide in His love. 11 "These things I have spoken to you, that My joy may remain in you, and that your joy may be full. 12 This is My commandment, that you love one another as I have loved you. 13 Greater love has no one than this, than to lay down one's life for his friends. 14 You are My friends if you do whatever I command you. 15 No longer do I call you servants, for a servant does not know what his master is doing; but I have called you friends, for all things that I heard from My Father I have made known to you. 16 You did not choose Me, but I chose you and appointed you that you should go and bear fruit, and that your fruit should remain, that whatever you ask the Father in My

Name He may give you. 17 These things I command you, that you love one another." (John 15:9-17)

I went through a very dark period in my early Christian walk that I experienced the powerful deception of the father of lies. I know very well the horror and tragic consequences of believing a lie. I experienced firsthand those who mishandle the prophetic gift and use it for personal gain.

I get why Paul wrote, do not despise prophecies. After experiencing such demonic, strong deception, I wanted nothing to do with any gifts of the Holy Spirit, especially prophecy. I didn't want anyone to ever prophesy to me again. I intentionally avoided the all-knowing, all-seeing hyper-spiritual Christians. I judged and labeled anyone who claimed to be a part of the Charis-maniac stream. I did what is known as 'throwing the baby out with the bathwater.' I blamed God the Holy Spirit instead of recognizing that people wounded through injustice by misguided authority are predisposed to become a bad example of power, that is unless they forgive, repent, and are healed.

I headed in the direction of becoming a Pharisee. My wound was so deep it affected the matrix of my soul, but, praise the Lord, the love of God ran deeper in me than the wounding. As the lyrics to "Unstoppable Love" by Mistry Edwards say it so beautifully.

Try to stop Your love, and You would wage a war.

Try to take the very thing, You gave Your life for

And You would come running, tear down every wall

All the while shouting, "My love your worth it all!"

God, You pursue me, with power and glory

Unstoppable love that never ends

You're unrelenting, with passion and mercy

Unstoppable love that never ends.

Thank God for His promise to *work all things together for good*. His love came after me, found me drowning in pain and rescued me! He won my heart by revealing from His Word, "...*there will always be tares growing with the wheat, until that day when they are separated.*" (Matthew 13:30)

Because of the profound darkness I experienced, I now have a deep respect for the Spirit of truth, as well as keen discernment when the angel of light is at work seeking to deceive the people of God. This deceptive spirit loves to use wounded hearts to create factions, contention, and discord. The victims of this spirit live to debate and wrangle over every jot and tittle (the letter of the law.)

They are blind guides who strain out gnats and swallow a camel! They do not know that the spirit behind what they do and say is a foul spirit using them to divide and create confusion among the innocent and those ignorant of the devil's devices. 1 Corinthians 11:18-19 "*For first of all, when you come together as a church, I hear that there are divisions among you, and in part, I believe it. 19 For there must also be factions among you, that those who are approved may be recognized among you.*"

This verse says the Lord uses factions so that those who are approved may be recognized. God's ways certainly are not man's ways. His kingdom is the opposite of what we would think. In His Kingdom, the way up is down. If you want to soar high, you got to go low. It's an inside out, upside-down kingdom. In the Kingdom of God, you lose to win and die to live.

We are exhorted not to quench the Spirit and despise prophecies, but instead, we are to test all things. The church needs to develop the gift of discernment in the testing all things. Unfortunately, when using the gift of discernment, people mistake judging the fruit and call it judging the person. Scripture is clear we are not called to judge the person, that is God's job. Only He knows the heart motives, intentions, and thoughts of man. We have the biblical responsibility is to test the spirit operating as instructed in the following,

1 Thessalonians 5:19-21, *"Do not quench the Spirit. 20 Do not despise prophecies. 21 Test all things; hold fast what is good."*

2 Corinthians 11:13-15, *"For such are false apostles, deceitful workers, transforming themselves into apostles of Christ. 14 And no wonder! For Satan himself transforms himself into an angel of light. 15 Therefore it is no great thing if his ministers also transform themselves into ministers of righteousness, whose end will be according to their works."*

Matthew 24:4, 24, *"And Jesus answered and said to them: "Take heed that no one deceives you. 24 For false Christs and false prophets will rise and show great signs and wonders to deceive, if possible, even the elect."*

Sad but true, many pastors don't allow the gifts of the Holy Spirit to operate in the church because they don't want to deal with the counterfeit. Many Christians have come to despise prophecy because a wounded believer, trying to cover over their wound with spiritual pride, operated under a pathetic gift instead of a true prophetic gift. Religious leaders often think it safer to shut down the Holy Spirit instead of dealing with a false spirit. They have believed a lie. Father forgive them, they don't realize they are resisting Your Spirit. Instead of trusting the Holy Spirit to give us discernment and wisdom, we grieve the Spirit by not permitting Him to speak through us or others who operate in the gifts.

The western church has paid a high price for such fear. We are void of the manifestation of the Holy Spirit gifts and the signs and wonders that were present in the early church.

2 Corinthians 2:4-5, *"And my speech and my preaching were not with persuasive words of human wisdom, but in demonstration of the Spirit and of power, 5 that your faith should not be in the wisdom of men but in the power of God."*

1 Corinthians 14:20-25 *"Brethren, do not be children in understanding; however, in malice be babes, but in understanding be mature. 21 In the law it is written: "With men of other tongues and other lips I will speak to this people; And yet, for all that, they will not hear Me," says the Lord. 22 Therefore tongues are for a sign, not to those who believe but to unbelievers; but prophesying is not for unbelievers but for those who believe. 23 Therefore if the whole church comes together in one place, and all speak with tongues, and there come in those who are uninformed or unbelievers, will they not say that you are out of your mind? 24 But if all prophesy, and an unbeliever or an uninformed person comes in, he is convinced by all, he is convicted by all. 25 And thus the secrets of his heart are revealed; and so, falling*

down on his face, he will worship God and report that God is truly among you."

Acts 7:51 *"You stiff-necked and uncircumcised in heart and ears! You always resist the Holy Spirit; as your fathers did, so do you."*

Before I go further, I want to share how I discern when the Spirit of God is speaking to me. I want to make my stand clear. I daily endeavor to align my life with the written Word of God. I do not receive, nor trust words spoken, either perceived in my own heart or through another, that does not…

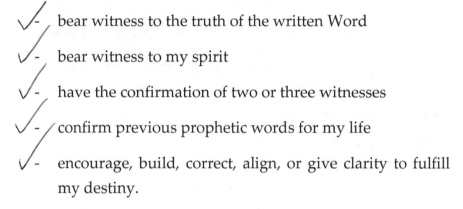

- bear witness to the truth of the written Word
- bear witness to my spirit
- have the confirmation of two or three witnesses
- confirm previous prophetic words for my life
- encourage, build, correct, align, or give clarity to fulfill my destiny.

When we have a sure word from the Spirit of God, it will give life to us and overflow to life others.

"It is the Spirit who gives life; the flesh profits nothing. The words that I speak to you are Spirit, and they are life. 64 But there are some of you who do not believe." For Jesus knew from the beginning who they were who did not believe, and who would betray Him. 65 And He said, "Therefore I have said to you that no one can come to Me unless it has been granted to him by My Father." 66 From that time many of His disciples went back and walked with Him no more. 67 Then Jesus said to the twelve, "Do you also want to go away?" 68 But Simon Peter answered Him, "Lord, to whom shall we go? You have the words of

eternal life. 69 Also we have come to believe and know that You are the Christ, the Son of the living God." (John 6:63-69)

God speaks to the human heart in a personal beautiful way.

- First and foremost, through His written Word.

- In a revelatory way that is gentle yet firm, He gives greater revelation of His nature, character and will to us.

- He speaks to our own heart through those who have faith to prophesy according to Romans 12:6, *Having then gifts differing according to the grace that is given to us, let us use them: if prophecy, let us prophesy in proportion to our faith.*

Looking again at what the prophet wrote in Habakkuk 2:1, *"I will stand my watch and set myself upon the rampart."* We must choose to stand our watch, and I am the one who decides to set myself upon the rampart. These are military terms that figuratively depict a watchman on the lookout for a word from God. I will watch and see what the Lord will say. We must, as the old saying goes, "stop, look and listen," or as my friend Dr. Negiel Bigpond says, "Sit down, shut up and listen."

How is it we can have ears but do not hear, and eyes yet do not see? The answer is in Scripture; our heart is stubborn and rebellious against the truth. Whenever we have a preconceived ideology, we are not open to hear and listen to what is said. The strongholds in our mind will predetermine whether we have a hearing ear. The following verses point this out clearly.

Ezekiel 12:2, *Son of man, you dwell in the midst of a rebellious house, which has eyes to see but does not see, and ears to hear but does not hear; for they are a rebellious house.*

Luke 8:8, *But others fell on good ground, sprang up, and yielded a crop a hundredfold. When He had said these things He cried, "He who has ears to hear, let him hear!"*

1 John 1:1-4, *That which was from the beginning, which we have heard, which we have seen with our eyes, which we have looked upon, and our hands have handled, concerning the Word of life— 2 the life was manifested, and we have seen, and bear witness, and declare to you that eternal life which was with the Father and was manifested to us— 3 that which we have seen and heard we declare to you, that you also may have fellowship with us, and truly our fellowship is with the Father and with His Son Jesus Christ. 4 And these things we write to you that your joy may be full.*

The Asbury Bible commentary explains Habakkuk 2:4 that by faith, the righteous person will remain loyal in his commitments to God regardless of the circumstances of his experience.

I remember when I was speaking at a Women's Aglow meeting, this mother came forward with her adult daughter for prayer. I asked, "How can I pray for you, ladies?" The mother responded on behalf of the daughter, saying, "My daughter has multiple physical disabilities and needs prayer." Being the simple woman of faith, I think to myself; she wants prayer for healing. So, I pray the Word of God in faith for her healing.

To my utter surprise, the mother got all worked up, raised her voice, and emphatically rebuked me, "She can't get healed, she would lose her Social Security Disability Insurance!" I was a bit surprised by the mother's response and calmly said, "Oh, I thought she wanted prayer for healing. I looked into the sad eyes of the daughter and directly asked her, "What is it, then do you

39

want prayer for?" Again, the mother answers before her daughter has a chance to, "She needs God's help to endure her suffering." So, I immediately asked God for wisdom for this awkward situation and prayed for the daughter that the Lord's mercy and loving-kindness would tenderly care for her need.

My heart broke for the daughter. Not just for her disability, but the emotional abuse she obviously suffered under her controlling mother. I thought to myself, "God help the pastor of the church they're attending. Lord, give the leaders wisdom and courage to pastor that special lady."

As sons and daughters of God, we are not to be lorded over by men or the spirit of this age. We live by the principles and standards of another Kingdom, whose government is ruled by another King, Jesus Christ. It matters not what news reporters, or the opinions of men say about us, about the issues of life or the future. What God says about the origin of life, the afterlife, current world events, gender, marriage, family, relationships, vocation, ministry, and finances is what ultimately matters.

I have learned the hard way, that when God speaks through a respected mentor in my life, it is not just a good idea that I listen, it is imperative I pay close attention. It is wise to take to prayer what is spoken, seeking the confirmation of two or three witnesses. When we receive wisdom from above, we then need to align ourselves with the directives. That, of course, is if I want to succeed in life and ministry. The choice is always ours. God does not superimpose His will on us. He invites us to be a part of what He is doing. That is not to say, as with Saul of Tarsus, that God can't show up and shove us off our high horse. After all, He is the Sovereign Lord!

Many of the opportunities God has invited me to be a part of I share throughout this book. I will never forget the first time I met Dr. Doug Stringer. It was a life-changing moment while having lunch with him and others at the July 2002 Call New York prayer gathering. Doug asked me to share what the Lord was doing in my heart and the city I was serving. With tears streaming down my cheeks into my salad, I shared with him my testimony of how the Lord used the first Sentinel Transformation video to break my heart with His heart for the lost. I shared the Scripture God used to speak to me that He was sending me as a prayer compassion missionary from Luke 10:1, (He) *sent them two by two before His face into every city and place where He Himself was about to go.*

I could not comprehend why the Lord would send *"Lil' ole"* me, who was raised in small towns, educated in rural schools, and attended a little country church. Why on earth would He send me as a prayer compassion missionary to an urban city? It seemed like worlds apart, and it was. I had zero understanding of inner-city life, but what I did have, they needed. I possessed the love of my Father, the peace of His Son Jesus, and had the testimony of the miracle-working power of the Holy Spirit. Isn't that what the world needs, love, peace, and the presence of God at work in their personal life? Miracles are for others to see Him at work, not just in us, which is our testimony, but also through us, which becomes their testimony.

I love the Travis Greene song, "He is Intentional." Everything God does is intentional and is not only for our good but for the good of others. Oh, how I love Him! He has a legit purpose for absolutely everything. One of the reasons I believe that God has called me to write is to leave a legacy, a lasting testimony of who He is to me personally and how He has flipped the script of what the enemy meant against me for evil and turned it for my good. The next generation needs to know there is a God who is alive and active in the affairs of humankind, and as Doug Stringer says, "It isn't real until it is written!"

That is one of the reasons while studying the Word of God; I journal what I am reading as I read it aloud, which helps me retain it. But the real test of the Word working in us isn't what we have memorized. We don't possess the Word until the Word possesses us. We act must act upon it by faith thereby exercising our spiritual muscles as the Holy Spirit works the truth into the matrix of our being.

James 1:22-25, *But be doers of the word, and not hearers only, deceiving yourselves. 23 For if anyone is a hearer of the word and not a doer, he is like a man observing his natural face in a mirror; 24 for he observes himself, goes away, and immediately forgets what kind of man he was. 25 But he who looks into the perfect law of liberty and continues in it and is not a forgetful hearer but a doer of the work, this one will be blessed in what he does.*

I wholeheartedly believe the reason so many believers are weak and impotent in their Christian testimony is that they only know the letter of the law, without the Spirit of the Word, which is the power to be His witness as recorded in Acts 2.

The following two Scriptures, apostle Paul writes, Romans 7:6, *But now we have been delivered from the law, having died to what we were held by so that we should serve in the newness of the Spirit and not in the oldness of the letter.* And 2 Corinthians 3: 5-6 *...but our sufficiency is from God, 6 who also made us sufficient as ministers of the new covenant, not of the letter but of the Spirit; for the letter kills, but the Spirit gives life.*

Without the Spirit of grace, we can be guilty of using the letter of the law wounding the soul instead of drawing people to God.

When I receive a prophetic word from the Lord, I write it down as I submit it to Him for confirmation. I don't act on it until He does. 2 Peter 1:19-21, *And so we have the prophetic word confirmed, which you do well to heed as a light that shines in a dark place, until the day dawns and the morning star rises in your hearts; 20 knowing this first, that no prophecy of Scripture is of any private interpretation, 21 for prophecy never came by the will of man, but holy men of God spoke as they were moved by the Holy Spirit.*

I appreciate and receive the fivefold ministry gifts that Christ has given to the church in my life and ministry. I invite all the gifts to minister at the church, as it says in Ephesians 4, to equip the saints. Not for one moment would I think that I can do anything without God's grace and gifts of the Holy Spirit. Ephesians 4:11-15, *And He Himself gave some to be apostles, some prophets, some evangelists, and some pastors and teachers, 12 for the equipping of the saints for the work of ministry, for the edifying of the body of Christ, 13 till we all come to the unity of the faith and of the knowledge of the Son of God, to a perfect man, to the measure of the stature of the fullness of Christ; 14 that we should no longer be children, tossed to and fro and carried about with every wind of doctrine, by the trickery of men, in the cunning craftiness of deceitful plotting, 15 but, speaking the truth in love, may grow up in all things into Him who is the head—Christ.* And then in 1 Thessalonians 1:5, *For our gospel did not come to you in word only, but also in power, and in the Holy Spirit and in much assurance, as you know what kind of men we were among you for your sake.*

There are distinct differences between churches as it has always been, so shall it be until the return of the Lord. You can read about the differences in the letters John wrote to the seven churches in Revelations 2 and 3. I will break it down into three main ideologies that differentiate them.

1) The *religious church* professes to believe the written Word, yet pick and choose what they believe, such as the fivefold ministry gift of apostles and prophets no longer exist, yet they believe that evangelists, pastors, and teachers still do. They believe the Holy Spirit baptism of fire was only for the early church as a one-time experience that is no longer needed to live out the reality of the New Testament church, which took the baptism of fire to birth it.

2) The *reprobate church* although they attend church they no longer believe the Bible applies to our modern day. They re-write, redefine, and challenge the Word according to their lifestyle preferences.

3) Lastly, the *remnant church*, those purified by Holy Spirit fire. Welcoming the anvil of God to fashion them to look, act, and live like the New Testament church in the book

of Acts. These believers align themselves with the Bible and welcome the Spirit of prophecy through holy men and women of God. The remnant church is the bride of Christ, those watching and waiting for the Bridegroom's return. Revelation 19:7-8, *Let us be glad and rejoice and give Him glory, for the marriage of the Lamb has come, and His wife has made herself ready. 8 And to her, it was granted to be arrayed in fine linen, clean and bright, for the fine linen is the righteous acts of the saints.*

I look forward to that glorious day when the Lord will return for His bride, the one purified by fire. I trust your prayer is as mine, "Whatever it takes Lord. make us ready for your return!"

Chapter 3

Broken for You

While watching the movie "Second Chance," the part in the film when the white man is washing the feet of the young black man, I wept. I can so relate to both the young black man, as one who has need of forgiveness, and the older white man who judged him. Both needing forgiveness and freedom from judgment is a sinful condition in every human heart. We all have the potential to condemn others, elevate oneself above others, and judge others' weaknesses. We read in Luke 10:30-37, the story of the Good Samaritan, who stopped to demonstrate love and care for his neighbor. We also see the same sad reality in our day, as the religious leaders of Jesus' day. Leaders who are too busy with ministry, full of pride, showing no mercy or compassion to their fellow man. If we are not mindful, prayerful, and careful, we have the potential to become just like the Pharisees. On the flip side, there is the practice of true undefiled religion, the disciples of Christ who...

- are obedient to follow His teachings and demonstrate His love

- choose humility

- give and receive forgiveness

- bless and do not curse

- live generous

I continually ask the Lord to make me sensitive to Holy Spirit conviction granting me the gift of repentance that causes godly sorrow, not the kind of tears common to all when we get caught and say we are sorry. Many as children learned using dramatic tears were like a get out of jail free card.

I am talking about the kind of repentance that breaks our heart over our own wretched, vile, offensive behavior that breaks God's heart. Without His loving conviction, when I violate His Word or offend the Holy Spirit, I can become a hardened, jaded, covenant-breaking, lawbreaker.

You know that kind of Christian the world reminds us is the reason they don't want anything to do with God or the Church. Yup, that kind of Christian, the one we sometimes see in ourselves (I mean those other people), in traffic, at the grocery store, on the job or at school. The judgmental, condescending, critical kind of Christian. Sadly, we all have the potential at any moment to become *that one*.

Jesus washed the feet of His disciples. It blows me away that among them was Judas, who would betray Him for thirty pieces of silver, and Peter, who would deny Him at a coal fire in front of a young girl. But Scripture says, He loved them to the end, and he called them His friends (John 13:1; Psalm 55:12-14). Despite what He knew about them, He washed their feet and invited them into a blood covenant with Him. Shukran Adoni (which is Hebrew for thank you Lord), for sending Your Son to die for us while we were still sinners!

How could it be? All twelve walked with Him for three and a half years. They saw the miracles, the healings, and the dead brought back to life. Yet, at the Passover meal, two of His disciples were about to fall. How could it be? Satan had influenced Peter and infiltrated Judas. Amid those holy, powerful, divine moments, I can easily see each of the twelve seated at that table, as a representation of today's Christian.

As a pastor, I am painfully aware of those in the church today as in biblical times who are offended, complainers, murmuring disputers, prideful, fearful, insecure, jealous, competitive and deceitful, (John 6:61; Mark 9:5-6; Matthew 8:26; Romans 12:3; 2 Corinthians 12:20). He stands at the door and knocks extending to us salvation, then we must continue to keep the door open to the Holy Spirit for healing and deliverance of our soul.

It seems clear to me why John was the only disciple at the cross with the women disciples. After all, John referred to himself as the disciple whom Jesus loved (John 13:23). He was the one resting his head on the Master's chest at the last supper and asked, *"Lord, who is it?" Jesus answered, "It is he whom I shall give a piece of bread when I have dipped it."* John was the one that Jesus revealed who His betrayer was. (John 13:26)

We are all invited to the Lord's table, and only He knows who the spots in our love feasts are. Jude chapter one warns us regarding the last days, false disciples will mingle among the true disciples of Christ, and that we will know them by their fruit.

Those who accept Christ's sacrifice on the cross are washed and cleansed by His blood. We are reminded of that sacrifice every time we partake of communion. His body broken for us; His blood shed for us. As we do this in remembrance of Him, how can it be that we still don't know we are His Beloved?

I believe the next two verses give some insight into why many find themselves praying for earthly desires, wants, and needs, over and over, without ever seeing a breakthrough. So many are not living as beloved sons and daughters. If we only had the revelation from Scripture that we are seated with Him in heavenly places and pray from the position of rest in the bosom (the heart) of the Father. John 1:16-18, *And of His fullness we have all received, and grace for grace. 17 For the law was given through Moses, but grace and truth came through Jesus Christ. 18 No one has seen God at any time. The only begotten Son, who is in the bosom of the Father, He has declared Him.*

I wasted years of my Christian life living in fear, insecurity and anxiety that is until the Lord opened my eyes. When my eyes opened, I chose to accept my place in the heart of my Abba, to rule and reign with Him in the hidden, secret place of His love. I was just like the two disciples in Luke 24, walking along the road to Emmaus, talking among them-selves, all the while, Jesus right there beside them, but they couldn't recognize Him.

It was not until they constrained Him and invited Him to abide with them as we read in the following verses.

Luke 24: 28-35, *Then they drew near to the village where they were going, and He indicated that He would have gone farther. 29 But they constrained Him, saying, "Abide with us, for it is toward evening, and the day is far spent." And He went in to stay with them. 30 Now it came to pass, as He sat at the table with them, that He took bread, blessed and broke it, and gave it to them. 31 Then their eyes were opened, and they knew Him; and He vanished from their sight. 32 And they said to one another, "Did not our heart burn within us while He talked with us on the road, and while He opened the Scriptures to us?" 33 So they rose that very hour and returned to Jerusalem, and found the eleven and those who were with them gathered together, 34 sayings, "The Lord is risen indeed, and has appeared to Simon!" 35 And they told about the things that had happened on the road, and how He was known to them in the breaking of bread.*

As the sons and daughters of Abba, we have a place at the table. He has seated us with Him in heavenly places. Unfortunately, not all will sit in the place prepared for them. When we serve in prayer with humility and confidence, we will see His power and authority at work in and through us to bring breakthrough. God calls intercessors not just to believe He can do miracles, but that He wants to use us to do them. The following verses encourage us of that place;

Job 36:5-7, Behold, God is mighty, but despises no one; He is mighty in strength of understanding. 6 He does not preserve the life of the wicked, but gives justice to the oppressed. 7 He does not withdraw His eyes from the righteous; But they are on the throne with kings, For He has seated them forever, and they are exalted.

Ephesians 2:4-6, But God, who is rich in mercy, because of His great love with which He loved us, 5 even when we were dead in trespasses, made us alive together with Christ (by grace you have been saved), 6 and raised us up together, and made us sit together in the heavenly places in Christ Jesus,

Luke 10:19-20, *Behold, I give you the authority to trample on serpents and scorpions, and over all the power of the enemy, and nothing shall by any means hurt you. 20 Nevertheless do not rejoice in this, that the spirits are subject to you, but rather rejoice because your names are written in heaven.*

And Matthew 16:19, *And I will give you the keys of the kingdom of heaven, and whatever you bind on earth will be bound in heaven, and whatever you loose on earth will be loosed in heaven.*

In Luke 4:18-19, Jesus declared the anointing upon Him to preach the Gospel with signs and wonders. It is His power and authority that sets at liberty those oppressed by demons, to heal physical infirmities and the brokenhearted. Then in Luke 9:1-2, He gives the disciples that same anointing and sends them out to do likewise.

He has blessed the church with every good gift to carry on His work, but the gift He still functions in heaven is, *Priest forever as Commander and Chief of Intercession* (Hebrews 7:24-25). When we are obedient to the Word to pray without ceasing, He will grace us with the gift of intercession as we are joined to and abide with Him in His ministry of prayer. Amazing isn't it; the Commander and Chief of intercession invites us to be His strategic weapon of love in warfare prayer? We get to join with Him interceding for souls, cities, and nations!

My heart is sad for Christians who live in the boring prayer zone. I have heard far too many believers say that after five minutes of praying for their personal needs, the weather, and of course, to find the best parking space at the mall, they are so done. They have not leaned into their Beloved, resting in His presence, soaking in His love, to hear His heartbeat for the world. I know that barren, empty place of prayer myself. It was my testimony before my heart opened to the beauty of Christ through communion. He sat at the table with them. He took the bread, blessed it, broke it, and then gave it to them. Following is how I apply what He did to my personal life.

- He took the bread; He took me out of darkness.

- He blessed the bread; He has blessed me with every good and perfect gift from above.

- He broke the bread; I needed Him to break me; to break my independent, self-righteous, stubborn heart and make my heart like His.

- He gave the bread: He gives us as a gift to the world as His prayer compassion missionaries.

He desires mercy and not judgment, and is lowly, kind, and humble. He is courageous and bold; I want to be like You! I give you my sinful nature in exchange for Your Holy nature! It is after the bread is broken He gave it. It is our brokenness that prepares us to be given as a minister of reconciliation.

I regard prayer and intercession among the most precious of gifts God has given the church. Ever since the day I watched the first transformation video in 1999, when He broke my heart with His love for the world, I love serving Him in intercessory prayer.

Prayer life's me, I know that's not a word found in the dictionary, but I use it anyway. It best describes how I feel when I pray. I feel alive, strengthened, encouraged, fired up, revived, and refreshed! One of the greatest joys I have is praying His Word over people, places, and principalities. I love to declare and decree what God's Word says, by calling those things that are not yet evident, as though they were.

I believe intercession is the calling of every believer. I refer to it as the "high calling" because it flows from the high place, the very throne room of God. It flows down to even the lowest place as David wrote in Psalm 139: 7-8, *Where can I go from Your Spirit? Or where can I flee from Your presence? 8 If I ascend into heaven, You are there; If I make my bed in hell, behold, You are there.*

Even when we find ourselves at the bottom of the abyss of sin and shame, the Lord will come to rescue us. He is not the least bit intimidated or afraid of hell because He conquered it. Jesus first descended to the lowest place. Ephesians 4:9 and Revelations 1:18 states, He took the keys of death, hell, and the grave before He ascended to His place far above principalities and powers, seated at the right hand of the Father. Only the risen Christ through the power of the Holy Spirit can go to the deepest, darkest place of the human soul, to rescue and deliver us from the power of the enemy, to restore and make all things new!

1 John 3:8, *For this purpose the Son of God was manifested, that He might destroy the works of the devil.*

Hebrews 7:25-26, *Therefore, He is also able to save to the uttermost those who come to God through Him, since He always lives to make intercession for them. 26 For such a High Priest was fitting for us, who is holy, harmless, undefiled, separate from sinners, and has become higher than the heavens.*

When God sent me to Haverhill in 1999, it was common to hear the city referred to as Hell's Hill. So as believers, we did what the Bible instructs us; we called dead things to life and called those things that were not, as though they were (Romans 4:17). We began to cancel out the decree of hell and declare that our city would be known as heaven's hill. We repented for the known sins of our city ancestors; we confessed we were poor in spirit, and we asked for the river of life to come and wash us. We asked for the healing waters that come from the high place to flow into the low place, the Merrimack Valley!

I believe we can apply God's Word on a personal level. I encourage you to read the following and put yourself in the middle of the promise. As you thank the Lord, know He hears the cry of your heart for the barren land you live in; call on the name of the Lord for your city and nation. He promises to give you living water whether you are on the heights, in the valleys, the wilderness, or dry land. Isaiah 41:17-18, *The poor and needy seek water, but there is none, their tongues fail for thirst. I, the Lord, will hear them; I, the God of Israel, will not forsake them. 18 I will open rivers in desolate heights and fountains in the midst of the valleys; I will make the wilderness a pool of water and the dry land springs of water.* He still brings living water from a rock!

The Lord will give a drink, a cup of cold water, to the thirsty, as mentioned in Matthew 10:42. When we drink from the river of God, our soul is satisfied. It is then His living water flows from us to others. In John 7:38, Jesus said, *out of our belly shall flow rivers of living waters* When we are connected to the very source of life, our lifestyle will bring a quickening, life-giving jolt like a defibrillator, to restore life to others. It will stir their soul to want His peace, His joy, and Holy Spirit power when we are living in such a way that others can tangibly see and experience Him.

Many years ago, I was given a prophetic word through Fran Lance. Fran was one of the founders of Women's Aglow. Following is a portion of what God spoke through her; "I have given you hind's feet and called you to a path that I have chosen for you, of which you cannot do with your regular shoes on, for I have called you to walk upon the high places with God." She then went on to quote Psalm 18:18-37 in the KJV.

As you read the following verses keep in mind Haverhill's nickname is Hillie's. How appropriate that the Lord would, spiritually speaking, give me the hind feet of a deer to walk upon the hills (the high places) to pull down strongholds in the name of the Lord. This is a word for every disciple of Christ living by faith amid the dark spiritual climate and depraved culture of our day.

> Psalm 18:28-37 (KJV), *For thou wilt light my candle: the Lord my God will enlighten my darkness. 29 For by thee I have run through a troop; and by my God have I leaped over a wall. 30 As for God, his way is perfect: the word of the Lord is tried: he is a buckler to all those that trust in him. 31 For who is God save the Lord? Or who is a rock save our God? 32 It is God that girdeth me with strength, and maketh my way perfect. 33 He maketh my feet like hinds' feet, and setteth me upon my high places. 34 He teacheth my hands to war, so that a bow of steel is broken by mine*

arms. 35 Thou hast also given me the shield of thy salvation: and thy right hand hath holden me up, and thy gentleness hath made me great. 36 Thou hast enlarged my steps under me, that my feet did not slip. 37 I have pursued mine enemies, and overtaken them: neither did I turn again till they were consumed.

Often, we find the journey long before we see the promise of God come to pass. We may find ourselves weary and discouraged in the waiting and asking the same questions as Habakkuk did in Habakkuk 1:2-3 (NIV). *How long, Lord, must I call for help, but you do not listen? Or cry out to you, 'Violence! But you do not save? Why do you make me look at injustice? Why do you tolerate wrongdoing?*

Habakkuk was a man greatly troubled by the horrific spiritual decline of his day. He desperately wanted to reconcile what he saw with his natural eyes with what he believed to be the truth. Sin and violence were rampant even among the people of God. He cries out to God, "Why?" Yet in the middle of chaos, he chose to rejoice in the Lord. Habakkuk giving the Lord thanksgiving was not dependent on circumstances. He gave thanks because of who God is, not because of what He does. In the following verse, he wrote about hind's feet as David did in the Psalms. Habakkuk 3:18-19 (KJV), *The Lord God is my strength, and he will make my feet like hinds' feet, and he will make me to walk upon mine high places. To the chief singer on my stringed instrument. Yet I will rejoice in the Lord, I will joy in the God of my salvation.*

A hind is a female deer that can place her back feet exactly where her front feet stepped. She can run with abandonment. In times of danger, she can run securely and not get off track. The hind can scale unusually dangerous terrain and elude predators.

God desires that we would run securely with abandonment and find fullness of joy in the Lord, regardless of our circumstances. In the natural realm, we may be facing what looks like a dead-end impossible situation. That is unless we see from our position by faith, seated with Him in heavenly places. It is then we have His shalom, the peace that passes all understanding. It is then we can see the situation as just another opportunity to use the mountain climbing hinds' feet. To watch His power rule and reign over the circumstance, trusting Him to work on our behalf.

When things look like they are going downhill or backward, often those on this journey with me have heard me say, to shoot an arrow, first, the archer has to draw the arrow back in the bow as he aims to release the arrow to hit the bullseye. It reminds me of Jesus; first, He descended before He ascended, and bam, like an arrow He hit the mark, once and for all!

If you have never read the book, "Hind's Feet on High Places" by Hannah Hurnad, I highly recommend it. Especially if you are finding the path difficult and a wee bit confusing as things may look quite different than what you believe God spoke to your heart. There is an appointed descent (backward or downward) before we ascent (forward or upward). We must learn to embrace His grace in what may appear to be a loss along the journey. For it is in the loss of all things we gain Christ, and it is in the struggle we learn to rule and reign with Him.

Ephesians 4:7-10, *But to each one of us grace was given according to the measure of Christ's gift. 8 Therefore He says: "When He ascended on high, He led captivity captive, and gave gifts to men." 9 (Now this, "He ascended" —what does it mean but that He also first descended into the lower parts of the earth? 10 He who descended is also the One who ascended far above all the heavens, that He might fill all things.)*

Philippians 3:7-11, *But what things were gain to me, these I have counted loss for Christ. 8 Yet indeed I also count all things loss for the excellence of the knowledge of Christ Jesus my Lord, for whom I have suffered the loss of all things, and count them as rubbish, that I may gain Christ 9 and be found in Him, not having my own righteousness, which is from the law, but that which is through faith in Christ, the righteousness which is from God by faith; 10 that I may know Him and the power of His resurrection, and the fellowship of His sufferings, being conformed to His death, 11 if, by any means, I may attain to the resurrection from the dead.*

I believe Scripture is clear, the Lord wants to do miracles through us, but until we have suffered the loss of all things, we cannot be trusted. He knows full well the temptation of the human heart to take the glory for ourselves. I love how the Lord sets us up for us to find what is hidden in our hearts. By divine design we are set up to discover, again and again, I can do nothing without Him.

It is after we suffer the loss of all things (such as pride, arrogance, insecurity, rejection, fear of man, and even success, that we can then be trusted for Him to work miracles through us. Mark 6:35-37*"When the day was now far spent, His disciples came to Him and said, "This is a deserted place, and already the hour is late. 36 Send them away, that they may go into the surrounding country and villages* *and buy themselves bread; for they have nothing to eat." 37 But He answered and said to them, "You give them something to eat."*

I love this; He knows we don't have the resources or the power to do what He asks of us. It is a setup for miracles by recognizing we have nothing and can do absolutely nothing without Him.

Romans 8:19 (NLT) *For all creation is waiting eagerly for that future day when God will reveal who his children really are.*

We are to be a vessel of His heart, voice, and hands to others in their time of need. Creation is waiting for the children of God to give them the same life-giving bread and refreshing water that He has freely given us, so they too may be satisfied in their thirst and hunger for truth. Psalms 46:7 declares God is our refuge, our high place that we run to in times of need. Our safety and security come from knowing and experiencing Him as our protector. Once we know Him in that way, the Holy Spirit compels us to invite others to know Him as Abba, Papa, Protector, and Defender.

In 1999 God sent a few of us to Haverhill, Massachusetts, to prayer-walk specific, targeted areas to intercede. At times He gave us insight before we prayed in a particular area, but that was not always the case. Sometimes it was after the Spirit of God led us to an area that had been decimated by crimes of injustice of every kind of depravity that we would receive the confirmation that what we prayed was accurate.

One such area we were sent on assignment was known as the "gateway to downtown." It was referred to as, where the low life gathered. The storefronts on that corner were just that, they were fronts for drug and prostitution operations. During one of my visits with the Chief of Police, he said to me, "Marlene that is no place for a lady to be." I thanked him for his concern for my wellbeing and replied, "It is where we are needed the most; we believe that the area can and will change with God's help."

God had far more in mind for us than to just pray on that city block. As we walked and prayed for eight years, we met the people who lived there as we picked up trash, needles, and filth. We passed out flyers inviting folks to the annual Somebody Cares New England (SCNE) summer block parties, winter holiday dinners, and giveaways as we built a relational bridge into the hearts of those living in darkness. Darkness is where the power of God's love shines brightest. In was in 2003 that we decided it was time to cast our vision for the city block and declare it as a "beachhead" of operations for the Kingdom of God. We added a picture of the storefronts on the corner of the intersection where we prayed, in the SCNE brochure.

Several years later, the owner of the building came across the brochure. After seeing the picture of his building on it, he threatened to sue us for false advertising and demanded we remove the photo or else! I humbly apologized, saying, "No harm intended, we were only trying to cast vision and invite people to pray." That did not help matters, and he only got more furious. We removed the picture from the brochure and continued to pray and love the block to life! Two years later, *boom shakalaka*, four storefronts opened for rent, all at the same time! We were so excited as us little donkeys trotted ourselves down to rent the space. The landlord (the same man that blew up at me years before) was delighted to rent us all four storefronts; we were a landlord's dream come true.

I love how God flips the script. I was now in the very building with the same man who threatened to sue us, with a lease in my hand. I thought, well, this is rather humorous. As I held back the chuckles, I just had to let him know. I am the crazy lady that you were going to sue for having a picture of your building on our brochure.

Although I thought it hilarious at the time, little did I know the price we would pay for taking over enemy territory. There were many things I was about to learn that I had not known before signing a three-year lease, that the landlord was probably having a good laugh to himself on us. But first, I want to share with you that at the very top of the high story building was etched in stone, *The Pentucket Building*.

There it was again, the original name of the city, the place of the long and winding river. God had opened the door for us to occupy the block, to establish a beachhead for Kingdom operations. There we were planted on the wall of intercession, to take back enemy territory and shut the gates in the very place known in the city as the gateway to downtown.

Let me be clear when I say enemy territory; it is not the people in that territory. I refer to the spirits that were given authority by innocent and ignorant people who were used by the antichrist spirit to rob, kill, and destroy lives. Now here we were, little donkeys, positioned by the highest authority to carry His light, love, and presence into the darkness, and that, my friend, is my idea of fun!

When we signed the lease, in my excitement, I must have overlooked the fine print stating there was no responsibility on the landlord, it was 'as is'. I had a surprise visit from five fire inspectors. They combed through the storefronts and came up with pages of code violations.

Violations that ended up costing thousands of dollars and two months of intense hard labor before we got a permit to move in. I came to understand the term, slum landlord. The owner had never done anything to this historic building, and the city of Haverhill saw us an opportunity to whack the donkey with the stick (codes).

 We shoveled cockroaches by the bucket full, (mind you, these storefronts were all retail stores and restaurants) before signing the lease. No other previous renters were hunted down by inspectors like we were. The sweet-spirited maintenance man that worked for the building owner for years just shook his head in disbelief of what the city was doing to us.

We found a trap door where the secret underground operations ran for as long as I could remember. One of our fun jobs was killing over twenty well-fed, fat rats in the basement. So, this was city life? The song that came to mind during our extreme makeover was, "Summer in the city."

Hot town, summer in the city,

Back of my neck getting dirty and gritty.

Been down, isn't it a pity,

Doesn't seem to be a shadow in the city

All around, people looking half-dead.

Walking on the sidewalk, hotter than a match head,

Cool town, evening in the city.

Dressing so fine and looking so pretty,

Cool cat, looking for a kitty.

Gonna look in every corner of the city,

Till I'm wheezing like a bus stop.

Running up the stairs, gonna meet you on the rooftop.

This song nailed it, including the rooftop, there was a penthouse, a shabby one, nonetheless, on top of this decrepit building. During this adventure I often had to remind myself, I had asked God to use me to do what I read in Isaiah 58:12, *And they that shall be of thee shall build the old waste places: thou shalt raise up the foundations of many generations; and thou shalt be called, the repairer of the breach, the restorer of paths to dwell in.*

Yup, God sent the little donkeys into such a barren place, just like the donkey in Tonopah, Nevada, that discovered the silver mines. There's silver (redemption) in *them there hills*! After years of plowing, sowing, watering, and loving the people in the low life area, God chose to move us from the "low" place in the city to a "high" place called Mt Washington.

The church we started in 2005, Community Christian Fellowship (CCF Ministries of Haverhill), was by a small band of prayer, compassion missionaries below ground level, in the basement of my home. It was here the leadership team met, of which I believe was prophetic. When you are going to build, the first thing one does is dig out the ground to lay the foundation with a basement.

For nine months, we dug up the fallow ground in the city through prayer and intercession. We studied together Dr. Daniel Bernard's book, "The Church at its Best," while we walked the streets doing what the Bible said, which is laid out in Daniel's book.

It was a historic day on November 5, 2005, when the prayer, compassion missionary team were anointed and commissioned to be sent out from the home church; CCF Ministries, located in Lowell, Massachusetts. In those early years, the Haverhill church plant was known as "CCF Street Church" as our motto was, "taking the love and power of Christ to the streets."

Several years after planting the church, I would often pray for the Lord to give us property and a building. As a sent one, I wanted to occupy the land and for our roots to be planted deep in the heart of the city. I wanted my life and time spent serving the Lord as a seed living on long after I am gone to be with Him.

As the ministry grew beyond just disenfranchised individuals to include families with children, we were also evolving into a church of beautiful diversity. We needed to move to bigger space that would be more conducive for the church to grow forward.

We started to cast vision and pray for a building long before we had the money for a down payment. But as God likes to prove Himself faithful, He did once again. The wisdom of man, of which I am not faulting, says no money, no building. The wisdom of God says, no money, no problem. If it is "God's will, then it is God's bill." Once the Lord has made known His will just start declaring that you have what you need and watch how miraculously provides. We did just that while we were praising and thanking the Lord for His provision, even though we did not possess it at the time.

One woman, who doesn't attend our church and lives in another state, believed in the mission God called us on. She donated $30,000 toward the down payment under one condition that we would raise the matching funds. Once people started hearing about the vision for a building and the $30,000 provision that already came toward it, we started receiving donations.

Checks came from other parts of the country, from some of the least likely people you could imagine, even from the low-income distressed population we were serving. The church was only five years old, and here we were, ready to move forward to purchase property.

A realtor friend of my husband was searching out property for us in the downtown area, but he could not find any within our budget. After some time, he contacted me about vacant property one mile up the hill located on Washington Street, called Mt Washington.

The street was named after President George Washington as he had visited Haverhill on November 4, 1789. Washington was on a "triumphant circuit," touring New England. Washington's impression of Haverhill was that it was "the pleasantest village he had passed through, with commercial advantages and beauty of the location." After he left Haverhill, the townspeople named its main meeting square, Washington Square.

(Haverhillusa.com)

I was not even remotely interested in going to look at a building that was for sale a mile away from the downtown area and up a huge hill. The realtor said, "Why do you have to be so stubborn, what's it going to hurt just to look?" Isn't that just like a donkey to be stubborn? He was so insistent I went just to appease him. When I walked into the vacant building, I was in utter shock and amazement at the despicable, horrific condition of this building that was built as a funeral home for the dead to make their last appearance for family and friends.

Who in their right mind would pay $350,000 for this nightmare? I asked the realtor to leave me alone in the building for a few minutes. Once he left, I witnessed the beautiful presence of the Lord, as I emphatically yelled out loud, "Are You kidding me? Is this the best you have for me? I was planning to have a testimony like some of Your other favorite ones. The ones that were given beautiful buildings by generous philanthropists for the furthering of the Kingdom, I would much prefer that testimony!"

Again, I found myself in the same scenario as downtown, a royal mess that God was going to use as a prophetic sign to this city. "Hello Haverhill, the people of God are here, sent to rebuild the old waste places and restore the paths (streets) to dwell in." It was then I was reminded of the old song by Ron Kenoly: "Going up to the high places."

We've been deceived,

By the devil too long.

We're gonna tear,

The devil's kingdom down.

What he said was his,

Has been ours all along.

We're gonna tear the devil's kingdom down.

God confirmed, as He always does when it is His will, and up we went to the high place, the top of Mt. Washington, to tear the devil's kingdom down. I was even more alarmed by the condition of the building as our electrician announced his findings. There were live wires in the attic! He said it was a miracle the place had not burned to the ground. The former owner, who at the time of purchase was President of City Council, had never done anything up to code. No wonder when we bought the building, he said, "Don't get the city involved, they will rake you over the coals."

No! Not again, yup again! Only this time, we were slapped with $75,000 of debt to bring the building up to code. I had hoped and prayed to move into a turnkey building. That doesn't seem to be the way the Lord likes to bring us, and I have since come to appreciate why. The difficult way has served to teach me His Word, His nature, and His beautiful ways in the process of restoration. Every single, challenging, hardship of the journey He has used for good.

Scripture tells us when God calls us to establish a beachhead of prayer, care, and share; predictably, the opposing spirit of the Kingdom of God will manifest. The following verse gives understanding; the enemy will often use those in the midst of us, the church, to not only speak against but try to stop the plan of God.

Jeremiah 29:7-9 And seek the peace of the city where I have caused you to be carried away captive, and pray to the Lord for it; for in its peace you will have peace. 8 For thus says the Lord of hosts, the God of Israel: Do not let your prophets and your diviners who are in your midst deceive you, nor listen to your dreams which you cause to be dreamed. 9 For they prophesy falsely to you in My name; I have not sent them, says the Lord.

There were several, even on our team that said, "This is not God, don't do it." One spoke out loud in front of everybody, "If you buy this building, you will not get one red cent from me, and I will not pick up a hammer to pound one nail." Well, all righty then, why not tell me how you really feel? When someone in their human wisdom, think they are wiser than God and resist what God wants, they are a candidate to learn a painful lesson about "kicking against the goads," from the Teacher Himself.

It was only a matter of time, which had nothing to do with me before the Lord separated those who opposed His will. To quote my pastor, apostle Najem, "Some are a blessing when they come, and some are a blessing when they go." I don't fault them for not seeing what I could see or for not believing the Lord's confirmation of His will to me. I feel bad for them; they honestly thought the Lord was using them. They were sincere, but as time did prove, they were sincerely wrong.

God knows we need personal revelation, especially when we are in over our head, in unknown territory. It wasn't until Joseph

(handwritten margin note: BE CAREFUL OF WHAT YOU SAY)

69

had a divine visitation did he accept that Mary's conception was God's doing.

> Matthew 1:19-21 *Then Joseph her husband, being a just man, and not wanting to make her a public example, was minded to put her away secretly. ²⁰ But while he thought about these things, behold, an angel of the Lord appeared to him in a dream, saying, "Joseph, son of David, do not be afraid to take to you Mary your wife, for that which is conceived in her is of the Holy Spirit. ²¹ And she will bring forth a Son, and you shall call His name JESUS, for He will save His people from their sins."*

Joseph was going to put her away secretly, that is, until he had a divine visitation from an angel that assured him. There is absolutely no way any of us can understand the plan and purposes of God unless revealed to us. Who He reveals it to and who He withholds revelation from is none of our business. Very often, it is a test of obedience on our part, not on those who are resisting.

God had much higher thoughts and plans regarding the strategic location He sent us. We had served the homeless in the downtown area for years, diligently working to get them off the streets. Now it was time for us to work on behalf of those who were in low-income housing to prevent homelessness. People need to have the hope of a better future as the following verse states in Jeremiah 29:11-13, *"For I know the thoughts that I think toward you, says the Lord, thoughts of peace and not of evil, to give you a future and a hope. 12 Then you will call upon Me and go and pray to Me, and I will listen to you. 13 And you will seek Me and find Me, when you search for Me with all your heart."*

70

God sent us up the hill, not just for the people we were serving, but for so much more. One sunny day while standing in my office looking out the window, it was as if I noticed for the first time, our property was on the corner of Washington and Shepherd Street. I felt the Lord speak to my heart, "I have placed you on this hill, on this corner as a prophetic sign. I have given you governmental and spiritual authority, and I will use you and this place to reach government officials and tear down strongholds over this city." God's thoughts and plans are not only higher, but they are also wider, deeper, and greater than ours! I would never think such audacious thoughts!

We have a sign as you enter the church greeting our first time guests; "Welcome to Haverhill the City of God, we have been waiting for you." The Lord has a special place in His heart for the first's; you can read it throughout His Word. We learned that Haverhill was a city of many firsts in America. I have listed a few that have equipped us with the prophetic insight of God's intent and divine destiny for this city. Haverhill was a forerunner city leading America in many firsts, to mention a few!

- It was the shoe industry that first made Haverhill's mark on the world. By 1811, 20,000 pair of shoes were manufactured a year. By 1830 production had grown to 1,500,000. In 1890, over 11,000 people were employed in the shoe industry, and that number continued to grow well into the early 1900s.

- Haverhill became a world leader in the shoe industry and was called the "Queen Shoe City of the World." At the shoe industry's peak, Haverhill had over 200 shoe establishments with a fine complement of support businesses (haverhillusa.com)

- It was this lowly city that led the shoe industry in our nation, preparing shoes for the feet of those who bring good news.

- The American Board of Commissioners for Foreign Missions was first organized June 29, 1810. Their purpose to commission missionaries to carry the Gospel to many lands, which has since ministered to millions through churches, schools, and hospitals.

- The first to establish a Christian school to educate girls preparing them for missions.

- Commissioned the first missionaries sent to a foreign land, Ann Hasseltine a Haverhill girl and her husband Adoniram Judson, as missionaries to Burma.

- First Macy's Day parade as it was home of the first Macy's department store.

- First in the nation to erect a monument in honor of a woman, Hannah Dustin.

Below is one of many pictures of the Somebody Cares team at the monument located in Bradford Square of Haverhill, Massachusetts.

From left to right, Sarah Stanley, Marlene Yeo, Dr. Jodie Chiricosta, Ashley Stringer, Dr. Doug Stringer, his wife Lisa Stringer, Katie, and Pastor Matt Stevens SC Baltimore, and Pastor Gideon Stanley.

How cool is that, God sent us as missionaries in the city of firsts! As is my habit of personalizing the Word I have added in parenthesis as it applied to us from Isaiah 52:7-9,*How beautiful upon the mountains* (the hills of Haverhill) *Are the feet of him who brings good news,* (we have shoes prepared to take the Gospel of peace to this city) *Who proclaims peace, Who brings glad tidings of good things, Who proclaims salvation, Who says to Zion,* (Haverhill the city of God you shall be saved)*"Your God reigns!" 8 Your watchmen shall lift up their voices,* (Your intercessors, the church of Haverhill, Massachusetts will be heard) *With their voices they shall sing together;* (with one voice) *For they shall see eye to eye* (as one people) *When the Lord brings back Zion.* (the missions' movement of Northpoint Bible College) *9 Break forth into joy, sing*

73

together, You waste places of Jerusalem! (Haverhill) *For the Lord has comforted His people, He has redeemed Jerusalem.* (Haverhill)

As intercessors, we must remind each other, the battle is not about us, or because of us, the battle is over the first. The firstborn and the first fruits. Following are three common strategies the devil uses to knock us out of the *good fight* of prayer and pull us into contention and strife, thus rendering us divided, powerless and impotent;

- When we are not fighting *together* against principalities

- We will fight *against* each other (flesh and blood which is personalities and ideologies)

- And *resist and offend* the Holy Spirit

Many do not know the testimony of Northpoint Bible College, formerly Zion Bible College, once located in Barrington, RI. Their history has collided with the spiritual heritage and prophetic destiny of Haverhill, Mass. None of us praying here in Haverhill, or those that were praying in Rhode Island, knew the Kingdom purpose God had in mind for the former abandoned Bradford Jr. College (founded as Bradford Academy.) The Lord was about to re-dig the wells of revival and birth intercessors, evangelists, pastors, prophets, and missionaries in preparation for the third great awakening in New England.

It was November 2002 when Dr. Doug Stringer came to Haverhill. He prophesied on the abandoned campus property and said, "Marlene, God wants you to gather the intercessors and pray to re-dig the wells of revival. From this campus, there will once again be missionaries sent to the four corners of the world." So in obedience, we started our prophetic, intercessory journey. God knows how I love adventures! From 2002-2007 we prayed on the campus every Monday, Wednesday, and Friday. Christian leaders, prayer warriors, and individuals came from all over New England and beyond to join us in prayer.

Our Haverhill Christian forefathers built and opened the school on this sacred ground. The historical documentation of the school can be read online in the book written by Jean S. Pond, "Bradford, a New England Academy." If you read this remarkable book, you too would have been compelled of the urgency to re-dig the wells of revival and pray for the rebirthing of the student mission's movement that started on this very property.

To quote from the book, "The emergence of a female benevolent network occurred at the same time that female academy movement was sweeping New England. In 1803 Bradford, A New England School named "Bradford Academy," was founded by a pastor and thirty congregants of the "First Church of Christ," establishing Christian education for their daughters."

In May 1806, a teacher that taught at the Academy named Abraham Burnham was used by God to start a revival on the campus that "even crossed the bridge" to ignite revival throughout the churches in the city.

It was in 1806 the Williamstown Haystack revival, where five young men who surrendered their lives to the call of God, birthed a student volunteer global mission's movement. In 1810 the establishment of a foreign mission's movement here in

Bradford Square, which was the American Commissioners Board of Foreign Missions (ACBFM).

In 1910, at the centennial celebration of the ACBFM, John R. Mott preached at the First Church of Christ. John Raleigh Mott, (May 25, 1865-January 31, 1955) was born as a pioneer for the Kingdom of God. He was a Noble Peace Prize winner, founder of the Young Men's Christian Association (YMCA), evangelist, author of sixteen books, he crossed the Atlantic over one hundred times and the Pacific fourteen times. John was chairman of the executive committee of the Student Volunteer Movement for Foreign Missions and presiding officer of the World Missionary Conference.

They said of John; he was a most trustworthy leader, one who adopts and applies guiding principles. He trusts them like the North Star. He follows his principles no matter how many oppose him, and no matter how few go with him. (Wikipedia)

While at the Bradford Common, John spoke these words, "The men that will change the colleges and seminaries here represented are the men that will spend the most time alone with God. It takes time for the fires to burn. It takes time for God to draw near and for us to know that He is there. It takes time to assimilate His truth.

Among other quotes of his, "The Church has not yet touched the fringe of the possibilities of intercessory prayer. Her largest victories will be witnessed when individual Christians everywhere come to recognize their priesthood unto God and day by day give themselves unto prayer."

The church members initially founded Bradford Christian Academy out of concern for their daughters. They wanted them to receive an excellent Christian education in preparation for the work of missions. I am grateful to the Lord for His call on the lives of women. It was sister Gibson, a woman who started the former Zion, now Northpoint Bible College. If God can use a donkey, He certainly can and does use a woman!

I have learned not to take it personal when people are opposed to women in ministry. I am not responsible for God choosing me. I'm only responsible for honoring and obeying His call on my life. After all, it was Mary Magdalene and the women, whom the angel of the Lord and Jesus Himself spoke to after He rose from the dead. He commissioned the women as the first to bring the Good news to the disciples!

> *Matthew 28:5-10, But the angel answered and said to the women, "Do not be afraid, for I know that you seek Jesus who was crucified. 6 He is not here; for He is risen, as He said. Come, see the place where the Lord lay. 7 And go quickly and tell His disciples that He is risen from the dead, and indeed He is going before you into Galilee; there you will see Him. Behold, I have told you." 8 So they went out quickly from the tomb with fear and great joy, and ran to bring His disciples word. 9 And as they went to tell His disciples, behold, Jesus met them, saying, "Rejoice!" So they came and held Him by the feet and worshiped Him. 10 Then Jesus said to them, "Do not be afraid. Go and tell My brethren to go to Galilee, and there they will see Me."*

I have come to appreciate and embrace the long and challenging process that God ordains for His dreamers. I apply the principles

I have learned from the life Joseph to my journey as a sent one to rescue lives. Genesis 37:5, 19, 20, *Joseph had a dream, and when he told it to his brothers, they hated him all the more. 19Joseph said to them, "Do not be afraid, for am I in the place of God? 20 But as for you, you meant evil against me; but God meant it for good, in order to bring it about as it is this day, to save many people alive."*

God has a dream that His Bride, the Church, will love Him and one another. Jesus prayed we would abide in the bond of oneness, love and peace. He desires us to pray His will on earth as it is in heaven. His Word says that all creation groans waiting for the sons of God to manifest. Ephesians 3: 10-12, *To the intent that now the manifold wisdom of God might be made known by the church to the principalities and powers in the heavenly places, 11 according to the eternal purpose which He accomplished in Christ Jesus our Lord, 12 in whom we have boldness and access with confidence through faith in Him.*

To end this chapter, I revisit the prophetic word from the Lord that I had 'Hind's Feet' and was to walk in high places of intercession. Fran also said it was a walk I could not do wearing my regular shoes. I needed to be fitted (shod) by the Master shoemaker with proper shoes to preach the Gospel of peace. To be one who preaches peace, I had to learn of the shalom peace of Christ that passes all understanding.

I see the absolute beauty of God's wisdom that He would call a hind (female deer) to intercede on behalf of a former girl's school campus established for women as missionaries. And that I would have the joy of seeing His dream come to pass and continue serving in prayer for Northpoint, a college founded by a woman, Sister Gibson, that equips missionaries to be sent to the four corners of the world!

Lest I mislead you, to think for a moment that everything we prayed all came to pass; I will end using a quote of George Allen. "I've prayed many prayers when no answer came, I've waited patient and long, but answers have come to enough of my prayers to make me keep praying on." *The Secret of Abundant Living*

Chapter 4

The Donkey Talks...Awkward!

On several occasions, people have said, will you pray for me, that I can pray like you, with power and authority? I know God hears your prayers, cause when you pray stuff happens." This one is my favorite, "I love it when you pray; I don't fall asleep." In this chapter, I testify of the power behind my prayers; it is none other than the Holy Spirit! When I received the Holy Spirit baptism of fire, it was then the Spirit of God began teaching me to intercede with the Word by the power of the Holy Spirit.

He will do the same for all who ask.

> Acts 10:34-39 *Then Peter opened his mouth and said: "In truth, I perceive that God shows no partiality. 35 But in every nation whoever fears Him and works righteousness is accepted by Him. 36 The word which God sent to the children of Israel, preaching peace through Jesus Christ — He is Lord of all — 37 that word you know, which was proclaimed throughout all Judea, and began from Galilee after the baptism which John preached: 38 how God anointed Jesus of Nazareth with the Holy Spirit and with power, who went about doing good and healing all who were oppressed*

by the devil, for God was with Him. 39 And we are witnesses of all things…"

We all can agree that God has never changed His mind about the great commission, the mandate is still the same. How is it then, that we think that we can obey it without the baptism of the Holy Spirit fire that empowered the first church in the book of Acts? Mark 15:16-18, *"And He said to them, "Go into all the world and preach the gospel to every creature. 16 He who believes and is baptized will be saved; but he who does not believe will be condemned. 17 And these signs will follow those who believe: In My name they will cast out demons; they will speak with new tongues; 18 they will take up serpents; and if they drink anything deadly, it will by no means hurt them; they will lay hands on the sick, and they will recover."*

So to set the record straight, If God can (and did), use a donkey to speak in a language that was not known to the animal kingdom, could that same God speak to this donkey and use me to speak in a language that is not a part of the language known to man?

We all have the same Holy Spirit available to us, as Paul writes in I Corinthians 14:14-15 *"For if I pray in a tongue, my spirit prays, but my understanding is unfruitful. 15 What is the conclusion then? I will pray with the spirit, and I will also pray with the understanding. I will sing with the spirit, and I will also sing with the understanding."*

We read in Jeremiah 18:2-4 *"Arise and go down to the potter's house, and there I will cause you to hear My words." 3 Then I went down to the potter's house, and there he was, making something at the wheel. 4 And the vessel that he made of clay was marred in the hand of the potter; so he made it again into another vessel, as it seemed good to the potter to make.* Verses 5-12 goes on to say the clay is marred, not because of the potter, but because of rebellion and sin. We have been marred and scarred by our sinful actions and the sinful actions of others done against us, yet as the verse states, we are in the hands of the potter.

The Bible reveals the Father's heart; He is always pleading with His people to repent. Repentance subverts the pending law of judgment for sin. The Lord would relent if only we would repent. All too common, the following is man's response to the Lord's mercy, as we read in verse 11-12, *"Return now everyone from his evil way, and make your ways and your doings good." 12 And they said, "That is hopeless! So we will walk according to our own plans, and we will every one obey the dictates of his evil heart."*

After salvation, the Lord begins the process of breaking the former image of a vessel marred by sin, to fashion us into another vessel, fit for the Master's use. Scripture calls that process sanctification, which is the means God uses to transform the human soul. It is a work of the Holy Spirit.

In some Christian circles, the Holy Spirit and His gifts are a dividing factor of churches. In many ways, it can be compared to the great divide over Christ the Messiah among Jews and Gentiles. We cannot escape the truth; it was the Holy Spirit outpouring in Acts 2, that the prophet prophesied in Joel 2, which empowered the disciples to turn the world upside down.

It was at Jesus' water baptism when the Spirit settled upon Him, and it was at that time John spoke of another baptism that would come.

Matthew 3:11-12*"I indeed baptize you with water unto repentance, but He who is coming after me is mightier than I, whose sandals I am not worthy to carry. He will baptize you with the Holy Spirit and fire. 12 His winnowing fan is in His hand, and He will thoroughly clean out His threshing floor, and gather His wheat into the barn; but He will burn up the chaff with unquenchable fire."*

 Matthew 3:16-17 *"When He had been baptized, Jesus came up immediately from the water; and behold, the heavens were opened to Him, and He saw the Spirit of God descending like a dove and alighting upon Him. 17 And suddenly a voice came from heaven, saying, "This is My Beloved Son, in whom I am well pleased."*

Many use this verse to support their belief that because Jesus did not speak in tongues when the Holy Spirit descended upon Him, neither do we need the baptism of the Holy Spirit with the evidence of tongues. To that, I would remind us, Jesus did not need water baptism as evidence of His repentance of sin, because He had no sin. Neither did Jesus need tongues of fire to purify His sinful nature. His baptism was to "fulfill all righteousness." Jesus was setting an example of obedience. When He did so, God affirmed that this was His Beloved Son through the evidence of the Holy Spirit saying, "This is My Beloved Son."

Sinful, offensive words of atrocity defile every language in every nation of the world. I am grateful to God for the language that comes from above. The heavenly language is not an offense to God, although it is an offense to the human mind. The heavenly language does not appeal to the intellect of man, and it cannot speak sinful words, because this sinful world cannot corrupt it.

The following are but a few reasons I value the gift of tongues. Before doing so, I want to clarify I am not talking about the gift of tongues operating through a believer in the public worship setting, as in I Corinthians 14. I am referencing the blessing every believer receives at the time of Holy Spirit baptism.

 Builds our faith, *"Building up yourselves on your most holy faith, praying in the Holy Ghost"* (Jude 20).

The Holy Spirit, who knows everything, can pray through us interceding for someone or something that our natural mind has no knowledge of.

 The devil has zero understanding of what we are praying.

It enables us to communicate spirit to Spirit with Him. *"For he who speaks in a tongue does not speak to men but to God, for no one understands him; however, in the spirit he speaks mysteries"* (1 Cor. 14:2).

 The Holy Spirit burns up the chaff, cleanses the mind and the heart of sinful words, foolish nonsense and fleshly thinking.

Praying in tongues grants access to other revelatory gifts of the Holy Spirit (1 Cor. 12: 8,10).

 It keeps us from getting distracted or telling God what we think He should do. Instead, we are agreeing with Him and what He wants to do. (Rom. 8:26-28).

Praying in tongues empowers us to engage in spiritual warfare from the position of victory.

- It does not ignore reality; it merely positions us in agreement with the higher truth of Scripture.

- Tongues reveal the wisdom of God, which confounds the wise.

- Praying in the Spirit edifies and builds up the believer. (1 Cor. 14:4).

- If I pray in an unknown tongue, my spirit prays. (I Cor. 14:14)

- When you speak in tongues, you are talking to Him by divine, supernatural means.

In the Old Testament story of the tower of Babel, God made a diversity of language to spoil and divide the evil plans of man. On the day of Pentecost, He gave us the one language of His Kingdom to unite His people to spoil and divide the plans of the enemy and to further His Kingdom plan.

The definition of Babel is a scene of noisy confusion of many voices, an uproar, a hullabaloo. God causes a hullabaloo to confuse the people because they are acting independently of Him. Is it not also very predictable that the counterfeit of God's Kingdom, the adversary, diablos, would cause a hullabaloo over the gifts of the Holy Spirit to confuse and divide the people of God?

The devil loves to divide the church over this issue with *concert*ed effort to provoke Christians against one another, so as to hinder the *concert* (concert: to arrange by mutual agreement) of prayer. God united the church together in one accord in the Upper Room, the high place, or the tower of prayer. He gave an unknown language for the birthing of the church, which can only be sustained by the power of the Holy Spirit. The devil has no new tricks, his plan is to get us offended with God and one another to keep us divided, and he will use Scripture to do it as he did with Jesus in the wilderness.

Matthew 4:5 *Then the devil took Him up into the holy city, set Him on the pinnacle of the temple, ⁶and said to Him, "If You are the Son of God, throw Yourself down. For it is written…*

In the modern sense of the word pinnacle is the golden spikes erected on the roof to prevent birds from settling there. This reminds me of Mark 4:3 that our faith will be attacked by the fouls of the air, with the intent to devour it.

Matthew 4:6" *…and said to Him, "If You are the Son of God, throw Yourself down. For it is written: 'He shall give His angels charge over you,' and, 'In their hands they shall bear you up, lest you dash your foot against a stone."*

Matthew 4:8-9 *Again, the devil took Him up on an exceedingly high mountain, and showed Him all the kingdoms of the world and their glory. 9 And he said to Him, "All these things I will give You if You will fall down and worship me."*

The adversary diligently works to divide man and God, husband and wife, parent and child, of which relationally overflows into the church. You can see the evidence of these divided relationships lived out in panoramic color in the church—the division between the pastor and the people and between the people in the congregation. We, who are called together in oneness, to worship and exalt Christ, to war in the spirit with prayer, to rule and reign with Him, and to work in the ministry together often find ourselves divided.

I have had non-tongue speaking Christians get angry at me for my belief about the gifts. My response to them is, "I am not angry or judging you for not speaking in tongues, why is it you judge me as deceived and are angry with me for speaking in tongues?" Speaking in tongues is not essential to go to heaven, although I believe it does have an essential role to live a victorious Christian life, my own life is proof of it. It would do Christians well to learn the motto of the Moravian Church; "In essentials, unity; in nonessentials, liberty; and in all things, love." Matthew 12:25 *Jesus knew their thoughts, and said to them, "Every kingdom divided against itself is brought to desolation, and every city or house divided against itself will not stand."*

Genesis 11:1-9 *Now the whole earth had one language and one speech. 2 And it came to pass, as they journeyed from the east, that they found a plain in the land of Shinar, and they dwelt there. 3 Then they said to one another, "Come, let us make bricks and bake them thoroughly." They had brick for stone, and they had asphalt for mortar. 4 And they said, "Come, let us build ourselves a city, and a tower whose top is in the heavens; let us make a name for ourselves, lest we be scattered abroad over the face of the whole earth." 5 But the Lord came down to see the city and the tower which the sons of men had built. 6 And the Lord said, "Indeed the people are one and they all have one language, and this is what they begin to do; now nothing that they propose to do will be withheld from them. 7 Come, let Us go down and there confuse their language, that they may not understand one another's speech." 8 So the Lord scattered them abroad from there over the face of all the earth, and they ceased building the city. 9 Therefore its name is called Babel, because there the Lord confused the language of all the earth; and from there the Lord scattered them abroad over the face of all the earth."*

The definition of a tower is to reach or stand high. In the context of this verse, it is safe to say; God used the Tower of Babel for division to destroy the works of man. Whereas, the Tower of Prayer, the Lord birthed on the day of Pentecost in the Upper Room, is for *construction* to build a Kingdom that cannot be shaken. Both scenarios involved language. When talking with Christians about the heavenly language, I will say, "So tell me, which of the languages known to man will be the language we all speak in heaven?" My Hispanics friends often jokingly say, "Why Spanish, of course!"

I proceed to my next point, "So a language that is defiled by foul and indecent words will be the language we all speak in heaven?" I think not! If our physical, decaying bodies that have been defiled by sin are not the bodies we will have in heaven, (we are getting a new one, praise Him), then why would any fifthly, defiled language be allowed in heaven? It will be a completely new language that He gives to us, and we can begin by using it here on earth, a pure language that is only known by heaven.

We pray, Your Kingdom come, but it already has, it is in us. We have the keys to the Kingdom, and we declare the Kingdom is here now!

Matthew 16:18-19 *And I also say to you that you are Peter, and on this rock I will build My church, and the gates of Hades shall not prevail against it. 19 And I will give you the keys of the kingdom of heaven, and whatever you bind on earth will be bound in heaven, and whatever you loose on earth will be loosed in heaven." Matthew 10:7-8 And as you go, preach, saying, 'The kingdom of heaven is at hand.' 8 Heal the sick, cleanse the lepers, raise the dead, cast out demons. Freely you have received, freely give.*

We love to sing and pray the lyrics from the song, "Our Father," by Bethel Music. May these words manifest in the here and now through us, the church!

Our Father in Heaven

Hallowed be Your name

Your kingdom come quickly

Your will be done the same

On earth, as it is in Heaven

Let Heaven come to earth

As it is in Heaven

Let Heaven come

Yours is the Kingdom; Yours is the power

Yours is the glory forever, amen

Psalm 81:5-16 *This He established in Joseph as a testimony, When He went throughout the land of Egypt, Where I heard a language I did not understand. 6 "I removed his shoulder from the burden; His hands were freed from the baskets. 7 You called in trouble, and I delivered you; I answered you in the secret place of thunder; I tested you at the waters of Meribah. Selah 8 "Hear, O My people, and I will admonish you! O Israel, if you will listen to Me! 9 There shall be no foreign god among you; Nor shall you worship any foreign god. 10 I am the Lord your God, who brought you out of the land of Egypt; Open your mouth wide, and I will fill it. 11 "But My people would not heed My voice, And Israel would have none of Me. 12 So I gave them over to their own stubborn heart, to walk in their own counsels. 13 "Oh, that My people would listen to Me, That Israel would walk in My ways! 14 I would soon subdue their enemies, and turn My hand against their adversaries.) 15 The haters of the Lord would pretend submission to Him, but their fate would endure forever.) 16 He would have fed them also with the finest of wheat; And with honey from the rock I would have satisfied you."*

Will we find ourselves, on that day, justifying the words spoken against our brother and sister in Christ who had an encounter with the Holy Spirit with the evidence of speaking in tongues? Will we continue to wrongly judge the gifts of the Holy Spirit by how wounded believers and insecure ministers use them as a means for self-promotion? Will we despise the gifts and working of the Holy Spirit in the earth today by calling what is Holy, strange fire?

Many years ago, I was one of those skeptics who mocked, ridiculed, and criticized the move of the Spirit in Toronto, Canada, until warned by my pastor, it is a fearful thing to judge or speak against what God is doing. I was one of three pastors from our church sent to the Toronto revival. Later on, in the book, I will share my personal testimony and how it forever changed me, and the youth ministry I was pastoring.

I can understand why so many are confused regarding Scripture. Without the Holy Spirit teaching us to divide the truth rightly, we will be wrongly divided by the truth. Without the Spirit of the Word to understand the Bible, we are left to our perceptions. We misinterpret Scripture and read into it what we already believe, instead of receiving from it what God has for us.

The following Scripture is case in point, we can be confused when we try to comprehend with our understanding. John 7:38-39 *"He who believes in Me, as the Scripture has said, out of his heart will flow rivers of living water." 39 But this He spoke concerning the Spirit, whom those believing in Him would receive; for the Holy Spirit was not yet given, because Jesus was not yet glorified."* John 20:21-22, *"So Jesus said to them again, "Peace to you! As the Father has sent Me, I also send you." 22 And when He had said this, He breathed on them, and said to them, "Receive the Holy Spirit."*

John 7 states, the Holy Spirit had not yet been given. John 20 states, He breathed on them and said receive the Holy Spirit. So how could they receive in chapter 20 when in chapter 7, it states the Holy Spirit had not as of yet come, and in Acts 1:4, they were commanded to wait for the Holy Spirit?

Yet before the outpouring in Acts chapter 2, they were able to cast out demons and heal the sick because Jesus had breathed on them before He sent them out. Mark 6:12-13 *"So they went out and preached that people should repent. 13 And they cast out many demons, and anointed with oil many who were sick, and healed them."*

These same disciples, although given authority to preach and do signs and wonders, still struggled with insecurity and fear, that is, until Acts 2, at which time they had another encounter with the Holy Spirit, the baptism of fire.

For many years I did not understand these different Holy Spirit experiences. John 20 was while Jesus was physically present with them as the Man/God when He imparted the Holy Spirit through His breath.

Acts 2 was after Christ ascended. This is when the Father baptized them in the Holy Spirit that was imparted by fire. When Christ walked with them as fully man and fully God, His breath and His presence was the power by which they did miracles. Interesting to note that although they did signs and wonders, their character never changed. It wasn't until after the baptism of fire, that Peter, who was afraid to confess he knew the Christ before the baptism is the same Peter who preached the day of Pentecost with Holy Spirit fire and boldness.

I had experienced God's breath, His Holy Spirit presence in my life, several years after accepting Christ while reading the book, "Nine O'clock in the Morning," by Dennis and Rita Bennett. It was then that my heart opened to receive the Holy Spirit. Although there was evidence in my life of His presence, the inner struggles deep in my soul were very much alive. The powerful transformation that I read about in the book of Acts that happened to Peter was not a reality in my own life, even though I knew I had the Holy Spirit.

It wasn't until many years later, when I experienced the baptism of Holy Spirit fire that I read about in the book of Acts that I understood the difference.

Acts 19:1-6 *And it happened, while Apollos was at Corinth, that Paul, having passed through the upper regions, came to Ephesus. And finding some disciples verse 2, he said to them, "Did you receive the Holy Spirit when you believed?" So they said to him, "We have not so much as heard whether there is a Holy Spirit." 3 And he said to them, "Into what then were you baptized?" So they said, "Into John's baptism." 4 Then Paul said, "John indeed baptized with a baptism of repentance, saying to the people that they should believe on Him who would come after him, that is, on Christ Jesus." 5 When they heard this, they were baptized in the name of the Lord Jesus. 6 And when Paul had laid hands on them, the Holy Spirit came upon them, and they spoke with tongues and prophesied.*

The Lord has more than the quickening of the Spirit that gives life at conversion or the infilling of the Holy Spirit breath in us; there is a Holy Spirit baptism of fire for those who are hungry for more. Jesus spoke before he ascended about the baptism of fire. If you are like me, you may be asking the same question I had. If they had already received the Holy Spirit when Christ breathed on them, as John 20:22 states, why did they need to wait for the Holy Spirit in the upper room, the high tower of prayer? Why? Because there is more and the more is not for our sake but the sake of the world, that we would be His bold, fearless, courageous witnesses to the ends of the earth!

Acts 1:8 *But you shall receive power when the Holy Spirit has come upon you; and you shall be witnesses to Me in Jerusalem, and in all Judea and Samaria, and to the end of the earth."*

More Lord! More of Your love, more of Your power! Baptize Your church in the fire of the Holy Spirit as on the day of Pentecost! There is more church! He wants us to ask for the more, not for our sake but for the sake of the world!

Luke 11:13 *If ye then, being evil, know how to give good gifts unto your children: how much more shall your heavenly Father give the Holy Spirit to them that ask him.*

Romans 8:19 *For the earnest expectation of the creation eagerly waits for the revealing of the sons of God.*

(CONTAINED WATER)

A) Filled w the Spirit seal for Salvation Your changed and blessed.

B) Baptized with the spirit you pour out what you recieved and others our blessed. (RIVERS OF FLOWING WATER)

FIRE → REFINES PURIFIES

95

Chapter 5

Tonto Goes to Toronto

Growing up, I loved to watch "The Lone Ranger" TV show. The crime-fighting adventures the masked man and his Native Canadian friend Tonto fought were exciting and heroic. Later on I will write in detail about my prayer journey with the Lord regarding the Native People. In the meantime, I want to make myself clear; the title of this chapter is in *no way* meant to be discriminatory against my native brothers and sisters. I am merely using it at times as an analogy and other times as an allegory.

First, for the millennials, a bit of background on the TV show that aired 1949-1957. "The Lone Ranger" is a fictional, masked, former Texas Ranger who fought outlaws in the American Old West with his Native friend, Tonto. The character has been called an enduring icon of American culture. The show generally depicted the Lone Ranger conducting himself by a strict moral code, which is based on truth found in scripture that reads:

- I believe that to have a friend; a man must be one

- That all men are created equal and that everyone has within himself the power to make this a better world.

- That God put the firewood there but that every man must gather and light it himself.

- In being prepared physically, mentally, and morally to fight when necessary for what is right.

- That a man should make the most of what equipment he has.

- That this government, of the people, by the people and for the people shall live always.

- That man should live by the rule of what is best for the greater number.

- That sooner or later, somewhere, somehow we must settle with the world and make payment for what we have taken.

- That all things change but the truth, and that truth alone, lives on forever, in my Creator, my country, my fellow man."

In one scene, the Texas Rangers had been attacked and killed, except one, known as the Lone Ranger, whose name was John Reid. It was then that Tonto is introduced on the scene and discovers the one Ranger barely alive, and he nurses the man back to health. In some versions, Tonto recognizes the lone survivor as the man who saved his life when they both were children. According to the television series, Tonto gave John Reid a ring with the name <u>Kemo Sabe</u>, which Tonto said means, "trusty scout."

Among the Rangers killed was the survivor's older brother, Daniel Reid, who was a captain in the Texas Rangers and the leader of the ambushed group. To conceal his identity and honor his fallen brother, John fashions a black domino mask using cloth from his late brother's vest. To aid in the deception, Tonto digs a sixth grave and places at its head a cross-bearing John Reid's name so that Cavendish and his gang will believe that all of the Rangers were dead. (Excerpts from Wikipedia.)

I can see the analogy in God's relationship with humanity. The enemy seeks to kill us, but God sends Jesus to rescue us. Not only does He rescue us and nurse us back to life, He spiritually buries our old man (covers us in the water grave of baptism), and gives us a new identity found in another, the Lord himself. That's not all. He provides us with a friend that sticks closer than a brother, a trusted scout, the Holy Spirit that rides with us through every adventure, protecting us from harm. Tonto recognizes the Lone Ranger as the one who saved him as a child. No act or word of compassion or kindness ever goes without the Lord's eye seeing or His ear not hearing.

As mentioned earlier, I was one who criticized the revival in Toronto. I found first-hand that people often criticize what they don't understand, instead of seeking understanding. Before sharing my testimony, some background of my life before I went to Toronto, Canada. I served as the youth pastor of a small group of Christian kids in a rural New Hampshire town for many years. Although the youth had come from good Christian homes, they struggled with debilitating fear, anxiety, and insecurity, as any typical teen does. Even though I was a more mature believer, I knew well the personal battle in my soul, resisting the same residual evils of my past life as a teenager.

Although I had repented, received forgiveness, and was not acting out my past sin in the same way as the teens, there was warfare just under the radar; I knew I was not free. When I would read John 8:38, "*Therefore if the Son makes you free, you shall be free indeed,*" I was missing the *indeed* part. The truth is Christ did set us free at the cross. But the reality, for me, was I had not yet experienced the resurrection power of the Holy Spirit. Before going to Toronto, I was not living out my faith walk from the place of freedom that I knew experientially. Therefore, I was unable to model for the youth, as well as for my children, what a victorious, joyful, humble, courageous, bold Christian life looked like, as I was not yet, free indeed.

I desperately wanted to see the youth set free, so I endeavored to gain an understanding of what the kids struggled with, to pray for them. I made a questionnaire handout for them to answer anonymously. I instructed them to be brutally honest and to write in block letters so as their handwriting could not identify who wrote the answers.

It worked, and I got more understanding than anticipated. Although I should not have been shocked by the typical teenage behaviors, as I too participated in the same actions as a youth myself, I was shocked because these were kids from Christian homes. My life choices were predictable for a teen raised in an alcoholic home with no knowledge of Christ. How could it be these Christian kids have the same struggles and behaviors that I did before I knew the Lord?

As I wept and interceded for them in prayer, my heart cried out, "Lord, deliver and rescue us all for Your name's sake, lest in the eyes of unbelievers they say, You are not able to deliver Your children." You can hear the similar conversation between God and Moses in Numbers chapter 14. God brought the children of Israel out of Egypt with His strong right hand. God used Moses' rod to open the Red Sea and swallow up their enemies. The Lord led them for forty years in the wilderness with miracles, signs, and wonders, yet they still did not believe or trust Him. On top of that, they continually complained about the journey and God's choice of leader.

Complaining is a grave sin that provokes the Lord's anger and tests His patience. Scripture says we reject the Lord's choice of the leader when we complain about them. The Lord told Moses He was going to wipe them out for their iniquity. A complaining spirit can become iniquity; the spiritual inheritance passed down through the family bloodline. I know because I was raised in such a family and trained as a skilled, professional, dedicated complainer. I could find a complaint against everyone and everything.

Moses and Aaron fall on their face to intercede on behalf of the murmuring, complaining people. We read in the following verses of the conversation between Moses and the Lord.

Numbers 14:5-24 "Then Moses and Aaron fell on their faces before all the assembly of the congregation of the children of Israel. 6 But Joshua the son of Nun and Caleb the son of Jephunneh, who were among those who had spied out the land, tore their clothes; 7 and they spoke to all the congregation of the children of Israel, saying: "The land we passed through to spy out is an exceedingly good land. 8 If the Lord delights in us, then He will bring us into this land and give it to us, 'a land which flows with milk and honey.' 9 Only do not rebel against the Lord, nor fear the people of the land, for they are our bread; their protection has departed from them, and the Lord is with us. Do not fear them." 10 And all the congregation said to stone them with stones. Now the glory of the Lord appeared in the tabernacle of meeting before all the children of Israel. 11 Then the Lord said to Moses: "How long will these people reject Me? And how long will they not believe Me, with all the signs which I have performed among them? 12 I will strike them with the pestilence and disinherit them, and I will make of you a nation greater and mightier than they." 13 And Moses said to the Lord: "Then the Egyptians will hear it, for by Your might You brought these people up from among them, 14 and they will tell it to the inhabitants of this land. They have heard that You, Lord, are among these people; that You, Lord, are seen face to face and Your cloud stands above them, and You go before them in a pillar of cloud by day and in a pillar of fire by night. 15 Now if You kill these people as one man, then the nations which have heard of Your fame will speak, saying, 16 'Because the Lord was not able to bring this people to the land which He swore to give them, therefore He killed them in the wilderness.' 17 And now, I pray, let the power of my Lord be great, just as You have spoken, saying, 18 'The Lord is longsuffering and abundant in mercy, forgiving iniquity and transgression; but He by no means clears the guilty, visiting the iniquity of the fathers on the children to the third and fourth generation.' 19 Pardon the iniquity of this people, I pray, according to the greatness of Your mercy, just as

You have forgiven this people, from Egypt even until now." 20 Then the Lord said: "I have pardoned, according to your word; 21 but truly, as I live, all the earth shall be filled with the glory of the Lord— 22 because all these men who have seen My glory and the signs which I did in Egypt and in the wilderness, and have put Me to the test now these ten times, and have not heeded My voice, 23 they certainly shall not see the land of which I swore to their fathers, nor shall any of those who rejected Me see it. 24 But My servant Caleb, because he has a different spirit in him and has followed Me fully, I will bring into the land where he went, and his descendants shall inherit it."

In 1994 while serving as a youth pastor, I was one of three of the four pastors on staff that went to "Catch the Fire" Pastors Conference in Toronto. It was there I first learned of Lou Engle, one of the speakers, a holy man that burns with the fires of intercession and revival.

The Toronto Airport Church and the 'so-called' revival that was happening caused a controversy that divided the body of Christ over its authenticity. As with anything the Lord is doing, the devil loves to smear it with overtones of soulish Christians who are just looking for a hyper-spiritual experience. The enemy likes to discredit what the Lord is doing through innocent and ignorant victims who operate in the flesh.

During the four day meetings with over 5,000 people from all over the world in attendance, I never experienced what I witnessed happening to others, of what was called the evidence of the Holy Spirit. What I can tell you though, is the testimony of my life-changing experience.

For several of the general sessions, I ended up alone in the overflow room watching from a distance on the Jumbo Tron. It was precisely where the Lord wanted me, away from the people I came with, all alone in a vast crowd, with just Him.

For three out of the four days, the Lord, in His mercy, brought forward panoramic scenes from my memory that unveiled my crippling attitude, critical spirit, and bitter root judgments, beginning as a little child. He blessed me with godly sorrow, remorse, and true repentance. Little did I realize at the time the gift those four days were for me. It was necessary to empty me before He could fill me with more of His love and power. His purpose for doing so was not just for me, but for the ministry, to be a carrier of revival back for the youth.

I left the conference different than when I had arrived. I felt like Caleb with a different spirit. At the time, I wasn't quite sure what the difference was; all I knew is that revival had come to my soul, and the revival anointing I saw and experienced in Toronto was about to break out and become evident in my life and ministry.

It was at that 1994 "Catch the Fire" Pastors' gathering that I heard Pastor Mike Servello Sr. and his wife Barbara's testimony. They had attended the pastors' conference the year before. It was then the Lord healed Barbara and delivered Pastor Mike from an intense spiritual battle. The oppression was so heavy that Mike wanted to quit the ministry and walk away from pastoring the church. They returned from Canada with an anointing that caused revival fire to break out in their church in Utica, NY.

I had previously heard of the Servello's through the prophetic ministry of Rita and Stephen Fedele, who were founding pastors and elders with the Servello's. Oh, the infinite plans of God! He is the designer of the net and originator of networking. He not only has a net to rescue the soul of every human being; He is the net that knits those same souls together for His Kingdom purpose! Little did I know when I met the Fedele's that in 1997 God was going to connect me with the Servello's for His Kingdom purpose!

So how do I know I was a carrier of revival anointing? You will know them by the fruit, and the fruit remained! There was a breakout of signs and wonders. Before leaving for Toronto, I had told my daughter that if there was a revival in Toronto, I was going to receive the revival anointing to bring it back.

I understood that anointing was transferable. As written in the Old Testament, Number 11:25 God took the same spirit (same anointing) that was on Moses and placed it on his elders. And in the New Testament, Jesus imparted the anointing to His disciples as written in I John 2:27. When I got back home, my daughter was so excited to hear about everything that happened. I did not tell her what I saw happen in Toronto for several reasons. I could not wrap my mind around it myself, I did not want to speak against it if it was the Holy Spirit, and I feared she would think her mother lost her marbles.

Our conversation went as follows, "Mom what did the Lord give you while in Toronto? I want you to lay hands on me and impart it to me." To avoid directly telling her anything I saw, I only told her, "All I got was the gift of repentance, I cried for three days."

I experienced Acts 3:19 *Repent therefore and be converted, that your sins may be blotted out, so that times of refreshing may come from the presence of the Lord.* Her response was so wise for such a young lady, "Mom, you can be a carrier of a cold without showing the symptoms of a cold, lay hands on me, I want the revival anointing."

So, I prayed a simple prayer of little faith, doubting that anything would come of it, "Lord, whatever you gave me, I impart freely to my daughter." Shortly after that, while she was enjoying a time of worship listening to a worship CD I brought home from the conference, suddenly, something supernatural happened to my little girl. I almost fainted as she manifested hilarious laughter as I saw happen to some people in Toronto. I knew that Proverbs 17:22 said, laughter does good like a medicine, but my experience of laughter, before the Toronto conference, was laughing at a funny joke or comedy movie. What I did not know then, is that God laughs at his enemies, Proverbs 2:4 and as I Peter 1:8 says in the King James, we could have unspeakable joy, and be full of glory.

This joyful laughter must be how Sarah felt, not the time she laughed in unbelief, upon hearing she would conceive and deliver a child beyond her childbearing age. I mean, the joyful laughter of unspeakable joy she must have felt in Genesis 1:6, after Isaac was born, when she said, *"God has made me laugh, and all who hear will laugh with me."* The dictionary definition of unspeakable means; exceeding the power of speech, unutterable, inexpressible, indescribable, intense emotion, and joy we are incapable of expressing with words.

In Toronto, I saw with my own eyes, people from every nation gathered for one purpose; they were hungry to know the Lord. I saw sincere desperation in these pastors; they wanted more of His manifest presence. In every language, they worshiped with abandonment, cried with joy, shouted loud praises, declared the greatness of our Lord, and did it with hilarious laughter and boisterous merriment. Now, here in my own home, my daughter was having the same experience, although I had not told her any of it.

Laughter breaks the spirit of heaviness and oppression; it causes light-hearted merriment like that of a little child without a care in the world. So many people are weighed down and have no joy, even in the church. Shouldn't we as Christians be the most joyful, celebratory people on the face of the earth? We have more reason than anyone in the world to be filled with unspeakable joy and be full of glory.

The Bible dictionary defines glory not only as of the magnificent, splendor, worth, and beauty of God's nature and manifest presence but also the beauty and bliss of heaven, a state of extreme happiness or prosperity. The definition of bliss in psychology is a state of happy and confident well-being sometimes exaggerated in pathological states as mania.

Or it may sometimes be, as John describes in Revelation, we may lay speechless as a dead man at the feet of Jesus in the overwhelming glory of His presence. At other times we may roll laughing with joy unspeakable and full of glory, thus the old-time expression, holy rollers. It would be safe to say, when we glorify and honor the King of Glory with our adoration, praise, and worship, we are then filled with His peace, joy, and righteousness.

I have seen very culturally reserved people, including New Englanders, who would think it blasphemous to fall over in hilarious laughter, do just that. They experienced a manifestation of His glorious, jubilant joy that cannot be uttered with words which renders one unable to stand and minister in His presence. I Kings 8:10-11 *"And it came to pass, when the priests came out of the holy place, that the cloud filled the house of the Lord, 11 so that the priests could not continue ministering because of the cloud; for the glory of the Lord filled the house of the Lord."*

What I saw with my own eyes in Toronto, I saw happen with my daughter, and I was about to see manifest in the youth ministry leaders. I called a team meeting, and without telling them what I saw in Toronto, we worshiped and then I laid hands on them and simply prayed as I did for Bethany, "Lord impart the anointing I received from the Holy Spirit, for the furtherance of Your Kingdom." We continued to worship and wait, and you know what happened? Even though I told them nothing, they experienced the same Holy Spirit baptism of joy!

We were all excited to see what would happen at our next youth service. After we worshiped, the youth leaders laid hands on each youth and simply prayed, "Lord impart the anointing you have given me for the furtherance of Your Kingdom." The Holy Spirit did it again. He filled the place with His presence; every youth was overcome by repentance, love, and joy of the Lord as the Holy Spirit fell on them all.

The floor covered with young people who were experiencing for the first time the conviction of the Holy Spirit that produced sorrow unto repentance. There was loud weeping over their sin, followed by the infilling of the Holy Spirit's power with joy unspeakable. Psalm 126:1-3 *"When the Lord brought back the captivity of Zion, we were like those who dream. 2 Then our mouth was filled with laughter, And our tongue with singing. Then they said among the nations, "The Lord has done great things for them." 3 The Lord has done great things for us, and we are glad."*

I remember the days before meeting the Lord when my friends and I would go out and have what we called a good time. What that meant was, get drunk, act like idiots, and laugh like fools. Didn't they say that of the disciples on the day of Pentecost? They thought they were drunk at nine o'clock in the morning, those drunken fools.

Definition of drunk, having faculties impaired, dominated by intense feeling, behaving improperly because of excitement, under the influence, effecting normal thinking and acting to become difficult or impossible.

So, what was this about? I will tell you *what it wasn't about*; it wasn't about just having an experience. *It was about the power of God* for the furthering of the Kingdom. Every youth service was filled with powerful worshipful experiences. Every week more and more youth were coming for the night of worship, experiencing the conviction of sin as their hearts converted to Christ in the presence of a Holy God. They were falling in love with the Lord and forsaking all others.

On their own accord, they asked for a bonfire to burn artifacts of things hidden in their bedroom. They brought their demonic music CDs, condoms, witchcraft books and whatever else they felt convicted to burn. They wanted their bedrooms to become a sanctuary of His presence for prayer. Ever since attending the conference in Toronto, our hearts were ablaze and burning with the fire of intercession and praying for revival. It was a sovereign move of the Holy Spirit. It was then I understood, Romans 12:11 AMP, "Be aglow and burning with the Spirit."

Young people started coming to the youth ministry as far as fifteen miles away because they heard, "God was in this place." They had a personal salvation experience, healing of broken hearts, and deliverance from strongholds. Young people testified that God spoke to them through prophetic words, dreams, and visions of His call on their life. Many were baptized in the fire of the Holy Spirit and became truth seekers and speakers. They were smitten by His presence and captured by His love. They became preachers of righteousness, holiness, and truth.

We saw firsthand the anointing that we read about in the book of Acts, the power of God setting captives free. Young people were coming to Christ every week. Youth ministry began to explode. We went from 15 youth to 150+ each week in our first year, and the adult leadership team grew to twenty-five. But again, it wasn't just about the experience. It was about furthering the Kingdom.

We developed several programs training the youth to use their talent for Kingdom purpose. One was called YITPA (youth in the performing arts). They were trained in choreographed dance, drama, mime, spoken word and music to preach the gospel with the arts. Also, we started the leadership training program, "Disciple's in Training" (DIT's), which had over 50 kids. One of the beautiful earmarks of the youth ministry was we were a joyful, happy, fun bunch. I can remember even back then saying to the kids, "I remind you all we are DIT's, donkeys in training, carriers of His presence into your school and remember all the glory belongs to Him!"

One special young man that the Holy Spirit led to our revival meetings was Darrell. He was a student at the same Christian school that my daughter Bethany attended. I somewhat knew Darrell, as I served as a devotions facilitator for the students.

He was an adventurous young man that was a wee bit edgy. I remember the first night Darrell showed up to one of our youth services. I jokingly said with a big smile, "Darrell Temple, are you here to start trouble?" I can still see the look on his face, when he responded with a sincere, humble voice, "I heard you guys have God in this place, and I need Him."

I was blown away by his sincerity. I knew God had something special planned for Darrell that night. We continued to do what we did every youth service since returning from Toronto. We worshiped using the CD's I had brought back. I preached a message about repentance, salvation, and Holy Spirit baptism of fire. We put worship music back on and lined up the kids who wanted prayer, which was all of them and pray we did! We prayed the kind of prayers that attracts the presence of God; they were desperate, sincere, simple, humble prayers of faith.

We asked for more! More Lord, we want more. More of Your love, more of your Holy Spirit power in our life, more of Your presence, fill us, Lord, with Your fire. We just wanted more of Him. He did a deep work in us all; our desire became His desire to see the nations come to know and worship Him! We prayed fervently, "Lord here am I, send me, use me," and He did just that!

Very soon after the new beginnings of revival fire, I took about twelve student leaders from our youth ministry team to the "Fresh Fire" youth conference in Toronto. It was there they got to meet, "the burning man," Lou Engle. This man burned with a holy fire of prayer and intercession like none I had ever seen. The session he preached was titled, the Atomic Power of Prayer and Fasting. It was then that the Holy Spirit anointed every one of us for the ministry of evangelism.

We knew what God had entrusted to us was to be freely given to others. Little did we know that what we were experiencing was going to have such a regional impact. After returning from that conference, we launched a student mission's movement, training youth as missionaries to their schools. We knew it would take a small army to pull off the vision, so we launched a six-month operation to prepare the students. We joyfully gave ourselves in continued prayer as we sought the Lord for strategy.

Some Saturday afternoons, we prayed upward of six hours, of which many testified of the great joy they experienced. None of us could believe how much time had passed; hours only felt like moments. Our leadership team invested themselves wholeheartedly in preparing and equipping the youth as missionaries to their high school campuses. After the intense training, we celebrated with a student-led, anointing, sending service on a Sunday morning. The congregation committed to pray for the youth as they were "sent out" as student mission-aries to their schools.

We invited Lou Engle to be our guest preacher for that amazing service, as he was the one God used to impart the anointing to the kids in Toronto. We commissioned them to go out to their schools in the love and power of the Holy Spirit. Every morning they gathered at the flagpole to seek the Lord. They knelt 30 seconds at their locker and prayed for teachers, students, and for opportunities to lead youth to Christ. They held student-led weekly Bible studies after school. They invited their friends to youth ministry and our bi-monthly regional outreach we called "Break Out Night," which was inspired from Micah 2:13 *"He one who breaks open will come up before them; They will break out, pass through the gate, and go out by it; Their king will pass before them, With the Lord at their head."*

'Break Out Nights' were mad, crazy, awesome, power-packed nights that got regional attention as the Lord drew as many as 500 young people. One of the teens that led an after school Bible study at Manchester High invited me to speak to the students at the Bible Club. The night before, she received a threat from the Satanists club that they were planning to cause a scene. Somehow a reporter from the Boston Globe got a "hot tip." No doubt in my mind, it was one of the Satanists looking for some ink. I love how the Lord flips what the enemy means for evil as an occasion for our testimony, as written in Luke 21:13-15 *"But it will turn out for you as an occasion for testimony. 14 Therefore settle it in your hearts not to meditate beforehand on what you will answer; 15 for I will give you a mouth and wisdom which all your adversaries will not be able to contradict or resist."*

The concerned young lady called to warn me, "Pastor Yeo, I think we better cancel tomorrow, the Satanist group on campus heard you were coming and have planned a rumble." I responded with, "Are you kidding me? I love a good rumble. I get pumped when I even remotely think of an opportunity to reveal God's love and power amid the enemy's plan. Whatever the Lord has planned for tomorrow, I am ready for it." Her response was, "I am not sure how many kids will attend; many of them are afraid to even come to school that day." I answered, "Well then, we have to show them what to do when a Christian receives a threat."

To my surprise, there sat a reporter for the Boston Globe that wrote for the New Hampshire section. She hung on every word as I preached a fiery message from the book of Daniel. I encouraged the few students who dared to come that day, how Daniel and his friends were a testimony of God's presence amid Babylonian culture. These brave young men didn't bend, they didn't bow to the demands to worship the king or the customs of their culture, and they didn't burn. They were not consumed by the fiery flames in the furnace, because they were already on fire.

> Daniel 3:24-27 *Then King Nebuchadnezzar was astonished; and he rose in haste and spoke, saying to his counselors, "Did we not cast three men bound into the midst of the fire?" They answered and said to the king, "True, O king." 25 "Look!" he answered, "I see four men loose, walking in the midst of the fire; and they are not hurt, and the form of the fourth is like the Son of God." 26 Then Nebuchadnezzar went near the mouth of the burning fiery furnace and spoke, saying, "Shadrach, Meshach, and Abed-Nego,*

servants of the Most High God, come out, and come here." Then Shadrach, Meshach, and Abed-Nego came from the midst of the fire. 27 And the satraps, administrators, governors, and the king's counselors gathered together, and they saw these men on whose bodies the fire had no power; the hair of their head was not singed nor were their garments affected, and the smell of fire was not on them.

The reporter sat there intently writing. She later expressed she was intrigued and wanted to know more about me and the youth ministry. She came to our next youth service and interviewed many of the youth about their faith in God and chose Darrell as one of them. She reported as best as could be expected, as one who wrote from a *not yet* Christian perspective. The story showed up on the front page of the New Hampshire section of the Boston Globe, yikes! We were now officially *out from under the radar*!

To quote one of my heroes of the faith, Pastor Jude Fouquier of Ventura, California, "You will know you are in true revival when the secular newspapers write about you, and the religious call you a cult." Tada, we qualified! It is too funny how the Lord will use the secular and the religious to confirm what He is doing. We were humbled and honored that God chose us little donkeys, the nobodies to be carriers of His presence into our Jerusalem.

Little did we know that God was going to expand our borders into Judea, Samaria, and the uttermost! To this day, I run into people who still comment on what God was doing in that region back in the early nineties. Romans 12:11 urges us to, *"Never be lacking in zeal, but keep your spiritual fervor."*

One will have spiritual zeal when one is spiritually ablaze. Weymouth translation is, "Have your spirits aglow; Godspeed, on fire with the Spirit"; and the Revised Standard Version states it, "Be aglow with the Spirit." What I experienced in Toronto was a personal Holy Spirit revival. He filled me with an abundance of His life, love, and zeal. He set me aglow to burn with the vibrant, radiant presence of the Holy Spirit.

He revived my devotion and obedience. I was no longer a "We can't do that; it's too radical, people won't like us, we don't have the money or enough people" Christian. He transformed me into a, "We can do that, God will provide, we only need a few, radical follower of Christ." I now trust in God's ability, instead of fear and my capability.

As Spirit-filled believers, we should be marked and known by intense, fiery devotion, eager willingness, and dedicated service to the King of the Kingdom we now belong. When the fire of the Holy Spirit burns within, and you live from a place of freedom and fullness, your inner life becomes radiant, your zeal intense, and your service unto the Lord is dynamic. As written in Ephesians 5:16, you will be *making the most of every opportunity.*

I went from seeing the cup half empty to not just half full, but to overflowing! I love it when I am in the center of God's will when secular humanist skeptics tell me that I can't do something because there is no money, not enough people, or too little time. Ha, ha, just watch Him use this little donkey; watch me whip, watch me nay, nay! Whip the opposition through obedience to the Word of the Lord. Listen to me, nay, nay to the naysayers. God had turned this once stubborn donkey into a persistent donkey, unwilling to settle for anything less than His absolute best!

Now, back to Tonto and the Lone Ranger. The announcer of the show would start with this introduction, *"A fiery horse with the speed of light, a cloud of dust and a hearty Hi-Yo Silver, away! The Lone Ranger with his faithful Native companion Tonto, the daring and resourceful masked rider of the plains led the fight for law and order in the early western United States. Nowhere in the pages of history can one find a greater champion of justice. Return with us now to those thrilling days of yesteryear! From out of the past come the thundering hoof beats of the great horse, Silver! The Lone Ranger rides again!"*

As you continue reading about the adventures of this donkey's journey, you will see how the Lord is transforming His lowly little donkey into His High Yeo Silver.

Chapter 6

Don't Beat the Donkey

If you don't know the story of Balaam, I recommend you stop here and take the time to read Numbers 22. It is the premise of this chapter. Let me preface by saying, this chapter is written not to hurt, but to help. I have weighed the risk of offending the reader before writing and believe it will be a blessing to those, who, too have been beaten for trying to rescue a life.

In Numbers 22, the children of Israel were taking over the land of Egypt. King Balak was afraid that if something didn't happen, the children of Israel would consume all of Egypt's resources. So the king hired Balaam, a prophet of God, to speak a curse over the people of God. Note it was the elders of Moab and the elders of Midian with the diviner's fee in their hand, who came to Balaam and spoke to him the words of Balak.

Balaam pleaded with God to let him go with the King. For the sake of my analogy, let's say Balaam represents those who believe their gift from God doesn't need to be submitted to authority, using their gifts for their profit and personal gain. The gifts of the Holy Spirit will operate by faith even though the one using the gift may lack the character of the Giver.

According to the dictionary, a diviner's fee is paid to someone to practice divination, to prophesy. I dislike that they mash the two words together, divination and prophesy. In the Biblical sense, they are diametrically opposed. Divination is rooted in the antichrist spirit of witchcraft and causes spiritual death, while prophecy is a gift given by the Spirit of the Lord and produces a blessed spiritual life.

As the story goes, initially, Balaam tells the princes of Balak, "Go back to your land, for the Lord has refused to give me permission to go with you." Ah, but the devil doesn't take no for an answer. Balak sends more numerous and more honorable princes to Balaam to plead with him to come; he promises to give Balaam honor. Balaam puts on a good show with 'religious lingo' saying, "I can only do what the Lord says to do, even if you offer me a house full of silver and gold."

I hear the religious of our day using the same spiritual line, "I can only do what the Lord tells me. I only go to a church when the Lord tells me; after all, I am the church." To that I say (to myself, of course), thank you, Lord, for exposing the religious spirit operating through that person. I do not claim to know what is in someone's heart, but I can and should discern what spirit is behind the words they speak. The Bible says, *out of the abundance of the heart the mouth speaks.* When necessary, the Holy Spirit will reveal, through discerning spirits or a word of knowledge what is operating through a person.

Jeremiah 17:9-10 *The heart is deceitful above all things, and desperately wicked; Who can know it? 10 I, the Lord, search the heart, I test the mind, even to give every man according to his ways, According to the fruit of his doings.*

God has prevented me many a headache and heartache when spiritual danger and emotional disaster tries to find me. I remember the day He revealed His wisdom to me from John 2:24 MSG, *But Jesus didn't entrust his life to them. He knew them inside and out, knew how untrustworthy they were. He didn't need any help in seeing right through them.*

I said Lord, "I don't know their heart and Your Word instructs me not to judge man's intentions." I felt the gentle correction of the Holy Spirit saying, "You don't know, but I do. I want to teach you to trust me when you get a witness in your spirit that something is off. I want you to guard your heart."

We can see from Scripture that Balaam was operating in his lower sinful nature, influenced by a spirit of greed. He invited the messengers to stay the night saying, "I will let you know what the Lord says in the morning." My spin on it, let me sleep on your offer; I will work on the Lord and see if I can get Him to change His mind.

I believe, based on biblical study, that there is the perfect, the permissible, and the passive will of God. It's not that God is permissive or passive. But what I do know first-hand, is that the Lord will let us go our own way and even allow words in the prophet's mouth to appear as confirmation, check it out I Kings 22.

I refer to it as His permissive will. If we persist in our ways, He will tell us what we want to hear, as He did Balaam, rise and go with them. I believe His passive will, is when we pray for

121

confirmation of a direction we want to take, and He is silent on the matter. It is as if He is saying, I am not even going to waste my time answering you. You are going to do what you want anyway. He knows full well we are only going through the appearance of seeking His will.

Isn't that what we want, our way? We may speak religious words that we want to do His will, but truth be known, we want, what we want, when we want it. Galatians 5 nails this behavior calling it witchcraft at work in the flesh. The Lord says to Balaam, you're going to do what you want anyway, so go ahead, but you will eat the fruit (suffer the consequences) of your way.

Isn't He wonderful that even when we choose to go our way, He is still with us? Oh, what a tangled web we weave because of the rebellion and stubbornness in our own heart. Oh, what needless suffering we put ourselves through because we are stubborn and willful.

I Samuel 15:23-29 *For rebellion is as the sin of witchcraft, and stubbornness is as iniquity and idolatry. Because you have rejected the word of the Lord, He also has rejected you from being king."24 Then Saul said to Samuel, "I have sinned, for I have transgressed the commandment of the Lord and your words, because I feared the people and obeyed their voice. 25 Now therefore, please pardon my sin, and return with me, that I may worship the Lord." 26 But Samuel said to Saul, "I will not return with you, for you have rejected the word of the Lord, and the Lord has rejected you from being king over Israel." 27 And as Samuel turned around to go away, Saul seized the edge of his robe, and it tore. 28 So Samuel said to him, "The Lord has torn the kingdom*

of Israel from you today, and has given it to a neighbor of yours,
who is better than you. 29 And also the Strength of Israel will
not lie nor relent. For He is not a man, that He should relent."
30 Then he said, "I have sinned; yet honor me now, please, before
the elders of my people and before Israel, and return with me, that
I may worship the Lord your God." 31 So Samuel turned back
after Saul, and Saul worshiped the Lord.

Serving as a minister of deliverance I am aware that many Christians live under the weight of the sin of stubbornness and rebellion. I have found most often, at the root of it is the fear of man. As Saul stated, he feared the people and obeyed their voice, instead of God (I Samuel 15:24). When we have the fear man instead of the fear of the Lord, it is a snare that will cause great suffering and grave consequences. We read that Samuel the prophet called out the spirit that Saul operated under in I Samuel 15:23 *For rebellion is as the sin of witchcraft, and stubbornness is as iniquity and idolatry. Because you have rejected the word of the Lord, He also has rejected you from being king."*

Even after God gives Balaam a perceived rite of passage, God continues, through other means, to try and stop Balaam from what would be a tragic ending. He uses a donkey to save his life and intercept pending judgment. All too often, like Balaam, we blame the donkey, striking out against the very people who try to help. As pastors, the intention and desire of our heart is to help people, yet sometimes people interpret it that we are unkind, judgmental, or lacking compassion. Often the sheep beat the pastor up (emotionally, verbally, and even spiritually) as Balaam did to his donkey. Ah ha, but God wastes nothing! He promises to use what is meant for harm as an opportunity for our good and the good of others.

Being raised as the oldest child and only daughter in an alcoholic family, I learned at a very young age; I was responsible for making everyone happy and fixing whatever was wrong. Not with words, but there was an encrypted, silent code deep in my heart. I somehow knew when things went wrong, it had to be my fault, and when things were right, it surely was my good behavior that must have caused it.

When raised in that kind of toxic environment, it can produce one of two responses, both of which are toxic at the root. One response is to act out in the same harmful behaviors done to us. The other response is to learn to overcompensate for the unhealthy behaviors. I am not sure what determines our response. It may be due to temperament or inner vows, but I fell naturally into overcompensating behaviors. I became a co-dependent enabler. One good thing that came of it is a compassionate heart, although before deliverance and healing, is distorted compassion. I never wanted anyone to suffer the consequences of their choices.

The problem with co-dependent behavior is that it sets one up to be manipulated, intimidated, and controlled by others who are dependent on your actions to make them happy. The fear of man is lurking in the deep, dark fiber of the co-dependents being. They live in constant terror that someone is going to be mad at them. If they don't do everything just perfect, that person you disappointed is just waiting to punish you. Therefore, your life-long assignment is to de-code everything they say and do. It is your job to figure out what they want before the hammer falls on your head.

If we turn on the news, we can see, in every sector of life, misappropriated authority taking advantage, abusing the weak and vulnerable. The truth is there will always be abusers and victims, but there is a way to stop the band from playing in your head and quit dancing with them. It is a painful process that can only begin when we allow the Lord to examine our own heart and how we play into the whole mess.

One of the most significant challenges I have found as a minister of compassion and reconciliation is to remain steadfast, immovable, and always abounding in the work of the Lord, regardless of people's opinions or how they treat or talk about you.

We must learn to be ok with the fact that we did the best we could at the level of wisdom and knowledge that we have at the time. We also must acknowledge we can always learn to do better. We cannot afford to allow the accuser to weigh us down with guilt, shame, and condemnation. In every accusation, there is a sliver of truth we can extrapolate from it. There is a verse that used to bother me; Matthew 5:25 *Agree with your adversary quickly, while you are on the way with him, lest your adversary deliver you to the judge, the judge hand you over to the officer, and you be thrown into prison.* While reading this verse in context and drawing the wisdom from it that God had for me, I meditated on Proverbs 15:1 *A soft answer turns away wrath, but a harsh word stirs up anger 2 The tongue of the wise uses knowledge rightly, But the mouth of fools pours forth foolishness.*

A religious spirit wants to draw us into a debate over every jot and tittle. It wants to prove you wrong, judge, and sentence you to a life in prison and make you indebted to your accuser. The only way out of that life sentence is to agree with your adversary quickly...what?

How can my accuser be right?

It's not about the accuser being right or winning. The accuser will always use a sliver of truth to build a case against you, agree with that sliver, and the argument ends. You cannot fight with someone that is right in their own eyes. A typical set up for disaster would be; the hurt, angry person accuses you saying, "You are selfish and self-centered; everything is all about you; you never listen to me!"

Careful, danger, danger! They just lit the match and are holding it a millimeter from your fuse. Your wrong response will set off the intended fireworks in panoramic color for all to see and hear! Don't bite the bait! The setup is for you to respond in defense, "Who are you calling selfish and self-centered? Yah, well you_____, blah, blah, blah! Fill your defensive response in that blank.

Wisdom from above teaches we are to come in the opposite spirit of an adversarial spirit. A wise response, would be apt to say is, "Thank you for sharing how you feel. I appreciate that. I will work on listening better. You matter to me, and what you say has value."

Why would one answer in such a way that gives the accuser the satisfaction of feeling they were right? Why? Because number one, we will use the opportunity to humble ourselves in the sight of the Lord. Number two, we win because we obeyed the wisdom found in Scripture. Number three, we can always agree with a higher truth than what is said. We can and should continually be growing in empathic listening, and this hypothetical example I just gave you my friend, is the perfect opportunity to do just that.

After all, there is a cloud of witnesses cheering us on to run without getting entangled. Arguing with a self-righteous person is a weight that can become a sin if we allow it.

Hebrews 12:1 *Therefore, we also, since we are surrounded by so great a cloud of witnesses, let us lay aside every weight, and the sin which so easily ensnares us, and let us run with endurance the race that is set before us.*

I love Heidi Baker, her ministry to the poor in Mozambique has had a powerful impact on me. I will never forget one of the stories she told about going into a native village to share the love of Christ, only to overhear them say she was on the menu for lunch.

She prayed, "Lord, they eat missionaries, and unless you do miracles, this is my last day on assignment in Africa, today I will be with you in paradise." She felt the Lord speak to her heart that He wanted to heal blind eyes and raise the dead, so, brave woman that she is, Heidi asked the villagers to bring their blind and deceased to her. The same Holy Spirit power that raised Jesus from the dead healed blind eyes, and many that were dead for several days came back to life. The Chief of the village, who was blind, was among those healed. The Lord not only miraculously saved Heidi's life, but the entire village accepted Christ.

When Heidi comes to America to minister, she says that it is harder to preach in the United States than in the darkest parts of Africa because of the spirit of witchcraft operating through religion in America. This spirit is evident in the very fiber of our nation. We are too educated to practice tribal witchcraft of cannibalism or the evils of the occult. But there is another kind of witchcraft, which Galatians 5 mentions as the work of the flesh.

This kind of witchcraft, although it opens the door to the demonic in the spirit realm, is found in the fallen nature of humanity. The MO (Mode of Operandi) of fleshly witchcraft uses manipulation, control, and intimidation to get ones' way at the expense of another.

The witchcraft that operates in flesh seeks to spiritually, emotionally, and mentally control others who stand in the way of their agenda. They oppose those who are pursuing the Spirit of grace and truth because this fleshly sorcery thrives on legalism and lies. Witchcraft and cannibalism are closely related; they both feed on others as written in Galatians 5:15, *But if you bite and devour one another, take heed that you are not consumed by one another.*

In nature, there are a few species that eat their kind. This phenomenon is considered an anomaly. Christians who engage in this practice are an abomination. The Greek word devour means to eat up, to consume by eating. I could never imagine such a depraved, disgusting thought. How can this be, that Paul would have to write to believers, not to devour one another, as it is a common practice among Christians?

Reverend Suliasi Kurulo, my friend from Fiji, told us about the move of the Spirit that brought revival to his nation. The spiritual and governmental leaders of Fiji humbled themselves, repented for the literal sin of cannibalism, and for spiritual cannibalism of division that was devouring the members in the body of Christ. Thank God for His loving kindness that brought them to repentance which broke the generational curses on their nation, and the blessing of revival broke out.

To this day, Fiji is being transformed in every sector of society. George Otis and the Sentinel Group have documented the proof that God has, does, and will transform nations. The evidence of a community, city, or nation in the process of transformation will manifest to some degree in all seven mountains or spheres of society: church, family, education, government, economy/business, media and arts or entertainment. I encourage you to watch "Let the Seas Resound" for yourself.

What I share next is a hard thing for anyone to understand with the natural mind; nonetheless, it is what Christ said to His disciples. Many walked away from Christ because of what He said because they were thinking with their natural mind.

> John 6:51-69 *"I am the living bread which came down from heaven. If anyone eats of this bread, he will live forever; and the bread that I shall give is My flesh, which I shall give for the life of the world." 52 The Jews therefore quarreled among themselves, saying, "How can this Man give us His flesh to eat?" 53 Then Jesus said to them, "Most assuredly, I say to you, unless you eat*

the flesh of the Son of Man and drink His blood, you have no life in you. 54 Whoever eats My flesh and drinks My blood has eternal life, and I will raise him up at the last day. 55 For My flesh is food indeed, and My blood is drink indeed. 56 He who eats My flesh and drinks My blood abides in Me, and I in him. 57 As the living Father sent Me, and I live because of the Father, so he who feeds on Me will live because of Me. 58 This is the bread which came down from heaven—not as your fathers ate the manna, and are dead. He who eats this bread will live forever." 59These things He said in the synagogue as He taught in Capernaum. 60 Therefore many of His disciples, when they heard this, said, "This is a hard saying; who can understand it?" 61 When Jesus knew in Himself that His disciples complained about this, He said to them, "Does this offend you? 62 What then if you should see the Son of Man ascend where He was before? 63 It is the Spirit who gives life; the flesh profits nothing. The words that I speak to you are spirit, and they are life. 64 But there are some of you who do not believe." For Jesus knew from the beginning who they were who did not believe, and who would betray Him. 65 And He said, "Therefore I have said to you that no one can come to Me unless it has been granted to him by My Father." 66 From that time many of His disciples went back and walked with Him no more. 67 Then Jesus said to the twelve, "Do you also want to go away?" 68 But Simon Peter answered Him, "Lord, to whom shall we go? You have the words of eternal life. 69 Also we have come to believe and know that You are the Christ, the Son of the living God."

If we do not feed on and drink from Christ to become like Him, we are vulnerable to become cannibalistic toward others. Every time we gossip, backbite, criticize, accuse, or slander a brother or sister in Christ, we are devouring them. That is to say, we are cannibalizing and demoralizing them.

There is a severe consequence for engaging in this abominable behavior. Cannibals are incredibly sick and have very short lifespans. The same is true of Christians who practice spiritual cannibalism; they become sickly and shorten the life span of their destiny.

This sin is subtle, and we justify what we do by calling it, being honest and telling the truth. Even when our attitude is non-verbal disdain for a person, it is the same as speaking evil of another. I have found that if someone talks about others to you, they will talk to others about you.

As Scripture says, the day is far spent and the night is upon us. It is high time for the church to unite and walk in love like never before. The spirit of slander, accusation, and offense has infected and divided the body of Christ far too long, and we have all been guilty. II Corinthians 2:9-11 *For to this end I also wrote, that I might put you to the test, whether you are obedient in all things. 10 Now whom you forgive anything, I also forgive. For if indeed I have forgiven anything, I have forgiven that one for your sakes in the presence of Christ, 11 lest Satan should take advantage of us; for we are not ignorant of his devices.*

Christ is returning for a glorious, pure bride, not a church of wolves and cannibals. Satan doesn't care how much we know about the Bible as long as we don't do what the Bible says. So, if we believe Scripture, that our words have the power to maim, hurt, kill, and destroy another's life, have you asked the Lord, why do we do it?

I believe one of the most significant reasons is unmet expectations. As Dr. Stringer says, "EDR, expectations destroy relationships." Scripture is clear; pride is behind strife, which often is just expectations or hope deferred that had made the heart sick. Proverbs 13:10, 12 *By pride comes nothing but strife, but with the well-advised is wisdom. 12 Hope deferred makes the heart sick, but when the desire comes, it is a tree of life.*

There is an old expression; you're only as good as your last deed. I have found this to be accurate, especially among those abused and neglected that become addicted to hurtful and harmful behaviors. They have a distorted view of themselves and others.

They see the world through the lens of brokenness. Many emotionally and mentally damaged from years of neglect and abuse as children, they have a high level of unrealistic expectations of others. Yet, they cannot live up to the expectations they superimpose on others. They expect someone to solve their issues, while their children look to them for help to solve theirs, of which, as parents, they are emotionally inept to do for their children.

There is a saying, hurt people hurt people, which is what keeps the cycle of generational sin and iniquity alive and well in a family bloodline.

Galatians 5: 1, 4, 7-10, 15-26 *Stand fast therefore in the liberty by which Christ has made us free, and do not be entangled again with a yoke of bondage. 4 You have become estranged from Christ, you who attempt to be justified by law; you have fallen from grace. 7-10… you ran well. Who hindered you from obeying the truth? 8 This persuasion does not come from Him who calls you. 9 A little leaven leavens the whole lump. 10 I have confidence in you, in the Lord, that you will have no other mind; but he who troubles you shall bear his judgment, whoever he is. 15-26 …you, brethren, have been called to liberty; only do not use liberty as an opportunity for the flesh, but through love serve one another. 14 For all the law is fulfilled in one word, even in this: "You shall love your neighbor as yourself." 15 But if you bite and devour one another, beware lest you be consumed by one another! I say then: Walk in the Spirit, and you shall not fulfill the lust of the flesh. 17 For the flesh lusts against the Spirit, and the Spirit against the flesh; and these are contrary to one another, so that you do not do the things that you wish. 18 But if you are led by the Spirit, you are not under the law.19 Now the works of the flesh are evident, which are: adultery, fornication, uncleanness, lewdness, 20 idolatry, sorcery, hatred, contentions, jealousies, outbursts of wrath, selfish ambitions, dissensions, heresies, 21 envy, murders, drunkenness, revelries, and the like; of which I tell you beforehand, just as I also told you in time past, that those who practice such things will not inherit the kingdom of God. 22 But the fruit of the Spirit is love, joy, peace, longsuffering, kindness, goodness, faithfulness, gentleness, self-control. Against such, there is no law. 24 And those who are Christ's have crucified the flesh with its passions and desires. 25 If we live in the Spirit, let us also walk in the Spirit. 26 Let us not become conceited, provoking one another, envying one another."*

I have found the adversary predictable with his aggressive strategy to demolish the ones who, like Nehemiah, are called by God to rebuild and restore. In Dr. Stringer's book, "It is Time to Cross the Jordan," he exposes how the enemy marks those who oppose his wicked plan to rob, kill and destroy them.

The religious spirits love money and will sell out God's people for monetary gain and fame even after hearing a clear word from God. Numbers 22:12 *"You shall not go with them; you shall not curse the people, for they are blessed."* The sin of witchcraft in Balaam's heart is what influenced him more than his respect, love, or fear of the Lord.

Three times his donkey tried to save him, as we read further verses Numbers 22:22-33 *"Then God's anger was aroused because he went, and the Angel of the Lord took His stand in the way as an adversary against him. And he was riding on his donkey, and his two servants were with him. 23 Now the donkey saw the Angel of the Lord standing in the way with His drawn sword in His hand, and the donkey turned aside out of the way and went into the field. So Balaam struck the donkey to turn her back onto the road. 24 Then the Angel of the Lord stood in a narrow path between the vineyards, with a wall on this side and a wall on that side. 25 And when the donkey saw the Angel of the Lord, she pushed herself against the wall and crushed Balaam's foot against the wall; so he struck her again. 26 Then the Angel of the Lord went further and stood in a narrow place where there was no way to turn either to the right hand or to the left. 27 And when the donkey saw the Angel of the Lord, she lay down under Balaam; so Balaam's anger was aroused, and he struck the donkey with his staff. 28 Then the Lord opened the mouth of the donkey, and she said to Balaam, "What have I done to you, that you have struck me these three times?" 29 And*

Balaam said to the donkey, "Because you have abused me. I wish there were a sword in my hand, for now, I would kill you!" 30 So the donkey said to Balaam, "Am I not your donkey on which you have ridden, ever since I became yours, to this day? Was I ever disposed to do this to you?"

It appears that Balaam's donkey was more spiritually discerning than the man of God. The sin of pride and greed in the prophet's heart blinded his spiritual eyes.

I remember when I answered the call of God on my life as a prayer compassion missionary. It was while serving as a youth pastor that I began taking the kids to the city of Haverhill with me. As we walked the streets and prayed, we *poured oil and wine in the wounds* of the lost and loved them to life. We started bringing the street people to the church. The parents expressed their concern that I was exposing their kids to inner-city issues and that somehow their child would be infected by the filth of sin. The leadership in the church did not understand what the Lord was doing, and how could they? While navigating through it back then, I didn't either. On top of it all, I lacked the confidence and assurance to communicate clearly and honestly, which made room for assumption and lots of misunderstanding.

I don't fault or blame the leaders; it was used to expose the co-dependent behaviors in my heart. I had sacrificially served this church for over twenty years with a proven track record of faithful obedience. As far as they were concerned, I was acting totally out of character. For several years the accusations flew around like locust on a crop of wheat. Finally, the day came when God made it clear it was time for me to leave; there is more to this story in my first book, "Where is God on Tuesday." It was during this time that some very hurtful things were said, such as, it was my pride that drew me to the people in the city because it made me feel important. The words that cut deepest were from the pastor, "I never really trusted you all these years."

I knew those words were not valid, as I recalled to him that for twenty years they had entrusted their children to my care whenever they traveled, I stayed in their home, and I preached in his pulpit. I was ordained by them and had faithfully served as an elder, youth pastor, and associate pastor. I knew they trusted me; what they could not do, was trust the Lord in me. I was a good, hard-working donkey that served well. I could relate to Balaam's donkey when he said, "*Am I not your donkey on which you have ridden, ever since I became yours, to this day? Was I ever disposed to do this to you?*"

When I left the church, I was not permitted to say goodbye to friends and the people I had served for twenty years. The last hoorah was when my former pastor called another pastor in the city I was sent to, telling him I split the church.

How do I know? The pastor in the city said he called to warn him about me. The accusation was unwarranted, when I left the church, I changed my phone number, email address, and even moved to another state. I went out of my way so no one could find me. Today I can see the purpose in all I went through. I can even joyfully smile now when I think about how the Lord has used it for my good, although it wasn't so joyful back then.

Those days were preparation for the soon coming challenge of being a church planter and lead pastor. I was about to learn some painful lessons from the Good Shepherd about the joys of pastoring wounded people. I would never have been able to gain such valuable lessons if a shepherd had not wounded me. Shukron Adoni, thank you, Lord! Thank you for always leading and loving me well, through the emotional wounding received in Your house by your people. I have learned from the Master of His agape love. Father forgive them for they know not what they do.

Chapter 7

Sent Out Before His Face

He called them out and then sent them out. The Lord spoke the following verse to my heart when preparing me to be sent out as a prayer compassion missionary.

Luke 10:1-4, 9-11 *After these things the Lord appointed seventy others also, and sent them two by two before His face into every city and place where He Himself was about to go. 2 Then He said to them, "The harvest truly is great, but the laborers are few; therefore, pray the Lord of the harvest to send out laborers into His harvest. 3 Go your way; behold, I send you out as lambs among wolves. 4 Carry neither money bag, knapsack, nor sandals; and greet no one along the road.*

9 And heal the sick there, and say to them, 'The kingdom of God has come near to you.' 10 But whatever city you enter, and they do not receive you, go out into its streets and say, 11 'The very dust of your city which clings to us we wipe off against you. Nevertheless, know this, that the kingdom of God has come near you.'

I understood why He sent them out two-by-two; by God's design, we need each other. I have found a world of difference between the friends in church relationships and the friends in the Kingdom relationships. We discover it through the test of time. I have found the average length of time most Christians are actively involved in their church is between three to four years. In our day, it has become the norm for believers to live out their faith relationally through technology. I know more professing Christians than I care to say, that don't fellowship in a local church. They profess to have relational problems in whatever church they attended and confess they are tired of trying. For sure, relationships are a challenge. I have even said to myself, "God and I are good, it's His kids I have a problem with."

Knowing the real story behind some Facebook pictures and posts, I am sad to say, many use it to put on a good face to the world. Kingdom relationships are different than church relationships. Those brought together by God for Kingdom purpose endure the test of time and survive misunderstandings and challenges that are normal in all relationships.

I am grateful to God for the Kingdom relationships I have. I am blessed to have so many Kingdom friends that have rejoiced with me in the good times and walked with me through difficult times. We dare to have those awkward, gut-wrenching, painful conversations when needed for our relationship to continue to grow.

Back to Luke 10, verse 2, He sends us out into the field to work and instructs them to pray for laborers. Prayer is a critical part of the mission field. Without prayer, there are no laborers and no harvest. The enemy will attack our Kingdom relationship to keep us from being obedient to pray together. We cannot let

140

different mindsets, models, and methods keep us divided over how or what to pray.

I found out very quickly the painful truth found in verse three. There are sly wolves that feed on innocent lambs, and they even go to church. They patiently lie, waiting to prey on the vulnerable and the weak. Several that God has brought into the church I pastor were preyed upon before becoming Christians by sex offenders, drug pushers, and pimps. Because of the injustice done against them, they struggle with thoughts of suicide as an option to escape their pain because they battle wicked, sinful thoughts. I am grateful to the Lord for establishing the deliverance and healing ministry, "He Cares for Me." We get to serve as His little donkeys to carry the broken out of the danger zone into safety through the ministry of prayer.

In verse four, I find it interesting the Lord sends out His handpicked leaders on a dangerous mission with no money bag, no extra clothes, or shoes. He instructs them not to talk to anyone and whatever city they go in if they aren't received, shake the dust from your feet, and keep going. That doesn't sound like a good church planting strategy. Again, Scripture reminds us, His thoughts and His ways are not like ours.

In Luke chapter nine, we read the Lord did not send them to start a church. Church planting is the byproduct, the fruit of preaching and demonstrating the kingdom. A Kingdom church plant is not necessarily with natural means of money and resources but with supernatural means, signs, and wonders that display the glory of the Kingdom of God and bears fruit that remains.

Luke 9:1-6 *Then He called His twelve disciples together and gave them power and authority over all demons, and to cure diseases. 2 He sent them to preach the kingdom of God and to heal the sick. 3 And He said to them, "Take nothing for the journey, neither staffs nor bag nor bread nor money; and do not have two tunics apiece."*

For years I could not understand why the Lord would do things contrary to what every good visionary starting a business, a ministry, or planting a church teaches. After all, aren't the three most important things to succeed: choosing the most visible, best location, gathering gifted people, and lots of money and resources?

That is, I didn't understand until I went with nothing. When I left my former church, my ordination credentials, my substantial paycheck was gone, my resources, my friends, and, most importantly, my pride of trusting in them shattered. I departed with nothing to rely upon except the Lord. It was then I learned some of the most beautiful lessons in my walk of faith. I learned it takes Kingdom authority to lay a foundation for Christ to build His church to advance the Kingdom of God.

Young people live in a culture flooded with supernatural phenomena of another kind. They don't find religious church services of interest if nothing supernatural is happening. They are hungry for preaching with power and authority, with signs and wonders following. They have little tolerance for organized religion; they want something real, raw, and relevant. Because I had nothing of my own to offer, I learned that whatever God provided by placing something in my hand was enough. I discovered the beauty of what Paul wrote in Philippians 4:11-13 *Not that I speak in regard to need, for I have learned in whatever state I am, to be content: 12 I know how to be abased, and I know how to abound. Everywhere and in all things I have learned both to be full and to be hungry, both to abound and to suffer need. 13 I can do all things through Christ who strengthens me.* It was during this time that I gained wisdom from my Teacher. I *learned*:

- Not to put my confidence in man, but to trust in the Lord

- Not to trust in anyone's promises to me, but to trust in what the Lord had promised in His Word

- Not to put my confidence in credentials, but in the calling and His anointing

- Not to put my hope in money, but to obey the great commission without any

- Not to judge others, because I too was judged wrongly

- Not to hold a grudge or want revenge, that is not the way of the Kingdom

- Not to hold onto un-forgiveness, because I also have need forgiveness.

Here is one such beautiful testimony of learning these lessons. The week before Resurrection Sunday, while talking with a few of the homeless at the day shelter, I asked, "What would you like to eat for dinner Sunday?" They had the look of shock as one man replied, "Nobody ever asks us what we want to eat; you're kidding, right?" After an awkward moment of laughter, I was surprised when one guy yells out, "I would love shrimp cocktail for an appetizer."

I thought to myself, holding back the chuckle, are you kidding me? That would cost a small fortune to feed the number of people we would be serving. And did I mention we didn't have a budget to buy anything, let alone shrimp and cocktail sauce?

I suspected the Lord had a surprise ahead for us all, a wink from heaven proving once again that He cares about every detail! I prayed, "Lord, You heard the request. Is shrimp on the menu for that day?" If so, we need a miracle equivalent, in my opinion, to the multiplication of fish and loaves. We positioned ourselves to watch and see in faith and you guessed it, shrimp cocktail was their appetizer.

The Lord used my husband to provide the miraculous, abundant supply. He was a policeman for 32 years. It so happened that week he was working overtime for the gas company. As they dug up the road for repairs, around the corner comes a seafood delivery truck. The driver hits a pothole, the back door swings wide open, and what flies out? Restaurant size boxes of shrimp across the road. The driver gets out, sees boxes scattered everywhere, looks at Harry, and says, "You know anyone to whom you can give these shrimps? I can't sell them now." Although the boxes were still tightly sealed, they were damaged and covered with grit and dirt. Harry gladly took them and delivered them to us.

If you could have seen the look on their faces that day as we served them shrimp cocktail appetizers in fancy plastic stemware. You can be sure I used that story on Resurrection

Sunday, as I told them, there is a God, He cares, and this shrimp is a reminder to us all, He still does miracles!

He is a good Father and provider. They had no problem with me praying to thank God for the food that day! That is just one of the over the top, hilarious testimonies. I have hundreds of them. Why? Certainly not because I am anything special. It is because I trusted God when I had nothing to give, except for what He provided. There is a saying I have; it comes from years of walking by faith, "If you are faithful to Him with nothing, He will trust you with something, if you are faithful with something, He will trust you everything,"

Again and again, God has confirmed it through several prophets. Pastor Brian Weeks and Pastors Stephen and Rita Fedele, to mention a few. The word they spoke by the Spirit was, "God calls you His friend, you have been found faithful in the fire. You have been tested with little and found faithful and will be trusted with much." The word of the Lord through Pastor Mike Servello Sr., "Marlene, because you care for the ones nobody wants, God is going to give you the ones everybody wants."

At first glance, that word seems demeaning, referring to them as the ones nobody wants. But the truth is, when the ones who have nothing come into the church, it is not uncommon they could be looking for a handout. They are not exactly the target population of most churches. Jesus said the poor will always be with you; many are born in poverty and will die in poverty.

I would not be exaggerating to say since planting the church in 2005 well over a thousand among the poorest in our city have walked through the doors of our church. Many came looking for someone to fix their mess, just looking for relief. Often people grow disappointed to learn of the hard work involved in changing their lifestyle, and they would just fade off in the distance.

Not everyone is ready to take responsibility and start the challenging process to increase the quality of their own life. But praise God because we love people unconditionally, and they experienced His love, some return to our caring community to start over again.

One such testimony is Flora; she was born in Uganda and came to America with the proper credentials. When her visa was about to expire, she chose not to return to her country. She had a good-paying job with a home health care provider but didn't let them know of her expired status. She lived in constant fear of the government. Years after attending our church, she was diagnosed with cancer and was in for the battle of her life. She became addicted to pain medication and would mix her meds with alcohol.

Because of her terrible choices and behaviors, her family had disowned her. Her life became even more complicated as she fell away from the Lord. We never lost touch during her crisis; we continued to bring her groceries and pray for her. She was so angry with God, blaming Him for the many painful things He allowed in her life. But finally, one day after she hit the absolute bottom, living in a homeless shelter, she started to reach out to God and reconnect with the church once again.

She made a new commitment to God, giving Him preeminence in her life, and slowly life started to turn around for her. She is now living in a lovely apartment, receiving the services she needs, and praise the Lord; she is completely cancer-free. Flora had said, "If it weren't for you, momma Yeo, I would be dead." I remind her, "Flora if it weren't for you coming back to Christ and doing the hard work it takes to make a life change, your right, you would be dead. I couldn't do any of that for you; I am only a little donkey that brought you groceries and carried you to God in prayer."

After Flora had become a stable, productive person again, she confided in me that during those painful years of recovery, she battled with resentment toward me. She wanted me to take her home to live in my basement. She thought it selfish of me that I had a house, and she didn't.

If I loved and cared for her as I said, I would have rescued her. As she told me of her anger, I just smiled and said, "If I had done that, it would not have solved anything. You had to learn through your suffering of the love and power of God for yourself through the process." Now Flora can see the truth, and her testimony is, God is her Savior, Healer, and Deliverer, not momma Yeo!

Yet, another testimony of God's faithfulness, when the Lord sent me out to the streets with nothing. Some said I was out of the will of God and that it would just be a matter of time, and everyone would see. As mentioned before, I am grateful to the prophetic Word of the Lord that Pastor Mike Servello Sr. gave me, "Because you will care for the ones nobody wants, God is going to give you the ones everybody wants."

Our pastoral staff is confirmation of that prophetic word. These incredible people would be on the most wanted list of any church staff. Among the eleven of us are those employed by the federal government, one works for Immigration and the other for Harvard Kennedy School of Government. We have three former Northpoint Bible College (NPBC) staff, (Dean of Students, office administrator, and professor of music and arts) and NPBC graduate who currently works as a social worker with the school system. One a licensed alcohol, and drug counselor director of a rehabilitation center, we have several entrepreneurs, a professional grant writer and last but not least, talented, skilled performing and creative artists.

I came across this hilarious quote that encouraged me along the journey. First is the original, then the misquote, which is just too funny not to share. Original by Nicolas Klein 1918,

"First they ignore you.

Then they ridicule you.

And then they attack you and want to burn you.

And then they build monuments to you."

The misquote;

"First they ignore you.

Then they laugh at you.

Then they attack you.

Then you win."

I have seen how God does this for the little donkeys. He flips the script and will even use the very accuser that once gave a false report about you. First, they call the donkey a loser, then out of their mouth for all to hear, God uses them to announce His little donkeys are the winners.

More than once, this scenario has played out, such as the day I was shaking out the front door mat at church. A woman that came to our food pantry stood at the bottom of the steps, smiling. After a pleasant greeting, out loud in front of God and the world she announces, "Marlene Yeo, they said you would never last in this city. They said you could never do it, but here you are, you showed them didn't you?" I laughed right along with her, "Bahahaha, I know right. The loser is now the winner!"

For the remainder of this chapter, I want to focus on Luke 10:1 *He sent them two by two before His face into every city and place where He Himself was about to go.* In March of 2011, while watching Channel 5, WBZ Chronicles, I almost fell out of my chair on the floor. I could hardly believe what I heard as I watched the thirty-minute documentary on Haverhill, Massachusetts, my city! It began with the Mayor saying, "Haverhill Massachusetts is a renaissance city in transformation." He said, what? At the end, Andre Dubus the author of the New York best seller book "Townie," which appeared to be the primary reason for the documentary, said, "It's wonderful to see a city that was once so full of darkness to now be so full of light."

All that is amazing and wonderful, yet something far more beautiful happened for me in the middle of the documentary.

Sharon Silverman, a local artist, had an art studio called Art and Angles. Sharon invited artists from across the globe to send the face of Jesus to display their artwork in her studio. They sent their art through the mail, thus its name, mail art. The pieces could be in any art form, with the stipulation, it was to be respectable, not rude or crude. At the time of the documentary, she had received from artists representing over 40 nations. To her delight, the face of Jesus arrived in a myriad of art forms that were on display downtown in my city! I heard Sharon say, "I have offered to display this collection of art from around the world in other cities, but they are not interested. They say it is too controversial, but Haverhill said yes to the face of Jesus!"

Although I had met Sharon many years before, it was seven years later when I contacted her to ask where the art was on display. She was disappointed that she had to put it in storage when she closed her shop. She was so gracious to take it all out of storage for display Holy Week at my friends, Rev Gene and Sandy Heacock's "House on the Rock." They dedicated this spectacular house to God as a prayer, presence and place of retreat in Gloucester, Massachusetts. Gloucester is one of the oldest art communities in the nation, and artists from across the globe come to Gloucester to paint. For the first time in years, the art was now being enjoyed and appreciated. In just four days, over four hundred people came through to view the many art forms of the face of Jesus. I then brought the collection back to Haverhill to once again be on display for four months in the church I pastor.

For several years I have been studying scriptures related to the face of Jesus. I have included a few of my notes. I first want to clarify that I have not seen the actual face of Jesus. I believe that we will see Him with our eyes, face to face, on the day of His glorious return. That is unless before then, we enter the portals of eternity through the door of death into His literal presence when we will see Him face to face.

The seeing I refer to is with the perception one has through spiritual eyes, which is not the same as human imagination with the use of images seen in pictures. The dictionary defines perception as the ability to see, hear, or become aware of something through the senses. Seeing the face of Jesus to me is when the tangible presence of the Holy Spirit is a personal, felt experience of His shalom peace and His closeness with the overwhelming awe of who He is.

When I receive a glimpse of Him, it always gives me greater insight and revelation of His glory, beauty, majesty, holiness, and His omnipotent, powerful love.

We are all on the journey of healing. Every human being has emotional needs that can only be met by the power of the Holy Spirit's continual transformation. It is as we look into the face of Jesus, asking the Holy Spirit to remove the veil over our heart and heal our brokenness, that we can then reflect the face of Jesus to others. For the disciple of Christ, the source of joy, peace, and righteousness can only come when we look upon the One we love. When we see Him, we become like Him. I John 3:2 *Beloved, now we are children of God; and it has not yet been revealed what we shall be, but we know that when He is revealed, we shall be like Him, for we shall see Him as He is.* The Holy Spirit draws us to look into the face of the Lord. His presence is the only place we will gain an understanding of our identity, worth, and value.

Sons and daughters of God are the reflection of the beauty of His face in the face of this dark fallen world. Even the devil knows that if he can draw us into looking at what is dark and evil, we will become like the darkness. The antichrist spirit wants to deface His face in us. Definition of the word deface; to mar the surface or appearance of, to disfigure, obliterate, destroy or injure as to make illegible or invalid. The devil wants to deface the walls or the boarders of your personality and prevent Christ from being seen in and through you.

- You are an original, created by God and no one in the entire world past, present, or future is like you!

- You are fearfully and wonderfully made. So then, why do so many live in fear and wonder why they are on this earth?

- It was in Genesis 2:7 that God breathed His life-giving breath into Adam's nostrils, God's mouth to Adam's nose. It is face to face encounters that give breath and life to humanity.

- Genesis 32:30b, Jacob said, *"For I have seen God face to face and my life is preserved."* It was after seeing God that Jacob's character and name were changed to reflect the nature and name of the One he saw.

- Exodus 33:11, Moses wrote, *"So the Lord spoke to Moses face to face, as a man speaks to his friend."*

- We draw our identity from looking into His face.

- Our confidence, stability, and security come from Him when we look into His face.

- We can be busy with our hands doing work for Jesus and be running with our feet to preach the Gospel, but none of that means we know Him face to face.

- If we are still and quiet in His presence allowing Him that place of intimacy (into me see), we will find the courage to confront the wounds that have marred, maimed, and marked us. Only when we are willing to deal with the pain that we can then begin to heal.

- When you look into His face, the image of His beauty changes the image we have of ourselves.

- The false image once projected upon us from sin and shame is shattered. As a result, we see our self differently. It is then we are free to live according to the image He has of us, then others will see His image in us and through His church!

- We may be able to walk away from we have heard about the Healer. We may be able to walk away from what we profess about the Deliverer. But it is harder to walk away from the Savior once you see His beauty.

I love the song, "Where You Are" on the Leeland Album "Better Word" (Live)

Oh I can't get enough

No, I can't get enough of

Your amazing love

No, I can't get enough

I can't walk away

No, I can't walk away

From where I've seen Your face

No, I can't walk away

I just wanna be where You are.

In the following verse, God told David to seek His face. Psalm 27:8 *When You said, "Seek My face," My heart said to You, "Your face, Lord, I will seek."* Man's deliverance from fear and shame comes from being in the presence of God. Psalm 34:4-5, *I sought the Lord, and He heard me and delivered me from all my fears. 5 They looked to Him and were radiant, and their faces were not ashamed."*

The people of God have a different spirit and the evidence is seen in their countenance. Our face reveals the peace and beauty of Christ. Numbers 6:24-26 *The Lord bless you and keep you; 25 The Lord make His face shine upon you, and be gracious to you; 26 The Lord lift up His countenance upon you, and give you peace.*

We read in the following text that when the Lord draws us near to Himself, we are on holy ground.

Exodus 3:4-6 *So when the Lord saw that he turned aside to look, God called to him from the midst of the bush and said, "Moses, Moses!" And he said, "Here I am."5 Then He said, "Do not draw near this place. Take your sandals off your feet, for the place where you stand is holy ground." 6 Moreover He said, "I am the God of your father—the God of Abraham, the God of Isaac, and the God of Jacob." And Moses hid his face, for he was afraid to look upon God.*

When we turn our face toward the Lord, we will experience supernatural peace to face our pain. He makes me lie down in green pastures and drink from still waters; He restores my soul.

When we lie down and are still in His love, He will embrace us and kiss our face with the kisses of His mouth. Song of Solomon 1:2-4 *Let him kiss me with the kisses of his mouth—For your love is better than wine. 3 Because of the fragrance of your good ointments, Your name is ointment poured forth; Therefore the virgins love you. 4 Draw me away! The Daughters of Jerusalem We will run after you. The Shulamite, the king has brought me into his chambers.*

In this life, we can only see a dim reflection, like a child with limited understanding, we only know Him in part as He reveals Himself to us. I Corinthians 13:11-12 *When I was a child, I spoke as a child, I understood as a child, I thought as a child; but when I became a man, I put away childish things. 12 For now we see in a mirror, dimly, but then face to face. Now I know in part, but then I shall know just as I also am known.*

As the song goes that Ron Kenoly sings, "The Lord Is Building Jerusalem," He is gathering together the outcasts of Israel, healing broken their hearts, binding up their wounds. Once we have the joy of deliverance from shame, fear, insecurity, self-consciousness, and pride, we can then enjoy the freedom to be who God designed us to be.

It was in the ninth hour that a certain man found this freedom.

155

Acts 3:1-10 *Now Peter and John went up together to the temple at the hour of prayer, the ninth hour. And a certain man lame from his mother's womb was carried, whom they laid daily at the gate of the temple which is called Beautiful, to ask alms from those who entered the temple; 3 who, seeing Peter and John about to go into the temple, asked for alms. 4 And fixing his eyes on him, with John, Peter said, "Look at us." 5 So he gave them his attention, expecting to receive something from them. 6 Then Peter said, "Silver and gold I do not have, but what I do have I give you: In the name of Jesus Christ of Nazareth, rise up and walk." 7 And he took him by the right hand and lifted him up, and immediately his feet and ankle bones received strength. 8 So he, leaping up, stood and walked and entered the temple with them—walking, leaping, and praising God. 9 And all the people saw him walking and praising God. 10 Then they knew that it was he who sat begging alms at the Beautiful Gate of the temple; and they were filled with wonder and amazement at what had happened to him.*

From that moment that man was free to dance, to move, to speak, and to live. It is then we are free to give to others what we have received. We can only give what we have fully possessed. Peter was able to provide the man maimed from his mother's womb that which he received when Jesus called him out of the boat. Matthew 13, we read that Peter started to sink when he put his eyes on the wind and the waves. He cried out, "Lord, save me!"

Jesus reached out, Peter took hold of the Lord's hand, and Jesus raised him to walk with Him. Many unborn are wounded while in the womb. The physical, emotional, and spiritual health of the mother, and the relationship she has with the baby's father, has a powerful impact on the well-being of the child's emotional state.

It was while reading the book, "Color Code," by Taylor Hartman that I learned of the importance of understanding our personality strengths and weaknesses. In Matthew 16 and Mark 8, we read about Peter denying his flawed character weaknesses. The Lord told Peter what was in his heart, but Peter would not listen to the truth, so the Lord allowed exposure of Peter's heart at a coal fire.

After the resurrection, Jesus recreated a similar scenario at a coal fire for Peter to have the opportunity to look face to face with the Lord, so that Peter could face what was in his heart all along. Because Peter faced his shame and painful memory of denying the Lord, he was then able to personally receive the Lord's mercy, forgiveness, healing, and restoration.

It was after that horrifying experience of denying the Lord that Peter preached on the day of Pentecost. In my human thinking, I would have chosen John, the beloved. After all, it was John, the only one of the twelve men, who remained with the Lord to the bitter end. It would make perfect sense, in my small-minded world, to reward John for his faithful dedication and sacrificial love. It blows my brain up, that regardless of our character defects and personality weakness, when we deal, we will heal, it is then we can co-labor with the Lord for His kingdom purpose. Once we repent, He baptizes us in His love and forgiveness, entrusting us as a steward of Holy Spirit power, to then preach the Gospel and lead others into freedom.

Becoming a healthy, competent person, parent, or leader is more about EQ (emotional intelligence) than about IQ (brain intelligence). It's about who one is, not about what one knows or does. Our identity center in the brain controls functions related to motivation, emotional stability, relational skills, ability to focus, how we care for others, our conscience, values, and the paradigms we have of life. Belonging and identity is the key to transformation.

Lasting transformation takes place when a person's identity is healed in the very presence of His love. Instead of living from a place of brokenness and shame, and we begin to live out our new identity from our position of love and acceptance. It is then that we grow up in Christ, living out our new identity as a son and daughter of God.

It is not until we have looked upon Him who was crucified and become skilled at handling the Word of life; that we can bear witness of what we have seen and heard. It is then we are empowered to be a witness to others. When we give our testimony, we offer others the opportunity to experience the power of His love and forgiveness personally for themselves.

People have the choice of whether to reject or receive the truth. Once a person repents and receives forgiveness from the Risen Lord, it is then we have fellowship with one another. Before salvation, there is no fellowship or communion (common union) with those living in darkness.

I John 1: 1-4 *That which was from the beginning, which we have heard, which we have seen with our eyes, which we have looked upon, and our hands have handled, concerning the Word of life—*

2 the life was manifested, and we have seen, and bear witness, and declare to you that eternal life which was with the Father and was manifested to us — 3 that which we have seen and heard we declare to you, that you also may have fellowship with us; and truly our fellowship is with the Father and with His Son Jesus Christ. 4 And these things we write to you that your joy may be full.

So, to recap, we are called out of darkness only to be sent out back into the darkness to testify as a witness of His light. Like John the Baptist, God sends us to proclaim and prepare the way for the Lord of the harvest. Luke 10:1-2 *After these things the Lord appointed seventy others also, and sent them two by two before His face into every city and place where He Himself was about to go. 2 Then He said to them, "The harvest truly is great, but the laborers are few; therefore pray the Lord of the harvest to send out laborers into His harvest.*

Although the world may look at us as being less than brilliant, as donkeys are referred to as dumb and stupid, on the contrary, according to Wikipedia, donkeys are quite intelligent. It is because of their stubborn stance they are stereotyped as stupid. But once they make up their mind, there is a slim chance of persuading them otherwise. This characteristic comes in handy when being sent out with nothing. We need *donkeytude*, the attitude that says, I am digging in my heels and I ain't moving come hell or high water, as written in I Corinthians 15:8 *"Lord, make me steadfast, immovable and always abounding in the work of the Lord that my labor is not in vain.*

Once we have seen Him face to face, we are persuaded, having found Him to be faithful, that He does keep that which is committed to Him until the day of judgment. (II Timothy 1:12)

Chapter 8

The Lost, Least, Little, and the Lonely

Seek and save that which is lost, Luke 19:10. In the spring of 1999, we began prayer walks in the Grand Army Republic Park, better known as GAR Park. Here is where the homeless gather under the cement dome. They gather to share in their woes, talk about their pain as they get wasted with alcohol, share joints, pills, needles, and their diseases with each other. It was November of that same year in the park that I met Donna.

She was a sight to behold, known as the most violent, drunk woman in the city. She downed a fifth or more of straight vodka daily. She was fearless in the face of men, including the police. I found her under a bush with no blanket, sound asleep on a cold winter morning.

She was startled by my presence, so after a brief introduction, I asked her when the last time was she had anything to eat. Her response broke my heart, "I can't remember the last time I ate." So I offered to get her some food and asked what she would like to eat. She said, "Nobody ever asks me what I would like. Who are you, and why do you care?"

I just smiled as I walked her to a cold cement bench. I told her to wait there, and I would get her request for pancakes, eggs, and hot coffee. When I returned, she had fallen over as if asleep again. So, I gently spoke to wake her. To my surprise, her eyes popped wide open as she said, "I wasn't sleeping, I didn't think you would ever come back. People tell me all the time that they will come back, and they never do." She kept asking, "Who are you anyway, and why do you care?"

As I fed her, being that she couldn't even hold the fork, I answered her question of who I was and why I cared. I told her that when I pray for the brokenhearted, I weep for them. I have offered myself for God to use me as His hands and feet. I pray here I am Lord, send me to the broken. He sent me here today, to you, Donna, just to let you know that He cares about you.

That day started a miraculous journey for us both. She taught me so much as we walked the road of transformation together. It blows my mind that God shares, in a small measure, the love that He feels for people with us. I told her that I loved her with God's love. She freaked out, saying, "How can you love me? You don't even know me?"

After a short time, she began to trust and love me as well. I am so grateful for the joy of leading her to accept Christ. I had the privilege to disciple her for the next eight years. I will never forget December 25, 1999; it was the day I led Donna in a prayer of salvation. It was no ordinary day at the homeless shelter; it was the day Donna confessed Christ as her Lord and received Him as her Savior.

The shelter is where the emotionally and mentally ill, alcoholics and addicts line up at five pm to secure a bed for the night. Men and women sleep the night in one big room of wall-to-wall bunk beds. It was the first Christmas day outreach that my children and twelve others from the youth group accompanied me to cook and serve Christmas dinner. We brought gifts that we bought and wrapped to give out to each individual. After the fun festivities, I preached a short message, "On the Road to Emmaus." It was the name of the shelter, "Emmaus," which was posted on the wall behind me with the Scripture Luke 24:5, "*So it was, while they conversed and reasoned, that Jesus Himself drew near and went with them.*"

I shared with them that just like the men written about in Luke 24, our sorrow and sadness is like a veil concealing His presence from us. We may not see Him, but He is there with us. At the end of the message, I gave an invitation for them to receive the gift of salvation. Donna was the first to respond. It was the best Christmas ever! We were not only blessed to give gifts, but we were also exceedingly blessed to introduce our Lord to these beautiful people who so desperately needed the gift of God's love and forgiveness.

Donna's testimony of her changed life reached the ears, eyes, and heart of all who knew her.

She was a different woman. She went to a detox center and worked all 12 steps of the AA program. She got a job and an apartment. Although it was challenging to face her painful past, she was willing. By choosing to do so, she began living with joy and peace on the journey of restoration.

Donna introduced me to Bill, the Director of *Community Action*. God used Donna, and the testimonies of other changed lives that accompanied our ministry to touch his life. I will never forget the look on his face the day he was a guest on the Somebody Cares New England TV show, as I asked, "Bill, can you say that Somebody Cares fulfills the mission we proclaim from Proverbs 14:25 "A true witness rescues lives?" He quickly retorted, "You can't rescue anyone; they have to recuse themselves!

Then almost immediately, as he sat there, he said out loud, "Hmmm, but then there is Donna, and Joyce and Annette, and all the others. They were not doing anything to rescue themselves. So, then I guess I have to say, yes. Yes! Somebody Cares does rescue lives." It is for testimonies such as Bill's that we, the Somebody Cares missionaries say, "Thank you, Lord, for the testimony that we are true to the mission!"

Unto the least of these, Matthew 25:40. In 2003, the church I was attending hosted an annual Christmas tea fundraiser that raised upward of five thousand dollars. The orphans in Africa and several single-parent mothers in Haverhill were chosen to receive the funds. Bill, from Community Action, gave me the names of the mothers so I could provide them with an invitation to be our guests of honor. At the fundraiser I introduced them and announced they would be the recipients of funds for their children's Christmas gifts, and the whole place broke out with cheers!

After the event, instead of dividing the funds, the elders decided that Haverhill was never a part of the mission of the church, and the single parents did not receive any funds for Christmas. Instead, the entire amount went to the mission in Africa. Although I was happy for the orphanage, I could not wrap my mind around what I was going to tell Bill. How was I going to cover the leadership's decision, so that Bill and the parents would not blame God for the church's misdirecting of promised funds? I was not only hurt by their choice; I was downright angry. I knew that my anger would not solve anything, and I did not want to complicate things.

Instead, I chose the high road of forgiveness as God directed me. I did not want to react in anger to this unholy mess, but to respond with a holy response and do what was right.

> Psalm 15:1-5 (NCV) "Lord, who may enter your Holy Tent? Who may live on your holy mountain? 2 Only those who are innocent and who do what is right. Such people speak the truth from their heart 3 and do not tell lies about others. They do no wrong to their neighbor and do not gossip. 4 They do not respect hateful people but honor those who honor the Lord. They keep their promises to their neighbor, even when it hurts. 5 They do not charge interest on money they lend and do not take money to hurt innocent people. Whoever does all these things will never be destroyed."

I withdrew the money from my savings and gave Bill a money order for the families. I never told him anything. It was eight months later, after I had already left the church, when I got a call from Bill, "I just received a check in the mail from your church.

In the memo, it said for Christmas gifts. We already received a money order last Christmas. Is this a mistake, should I return the check?" I did my best to cover things without lying, but I was humiliated by the church. I told Bill to keep the funds to use for next Christmas for families in need of assistance.

Is it any wonder our testimony to the world is so weak? It reminds me of a quote from Gandhi, "I like your Christ; I do not like your Christians. Your Christians are so unlike your Christ." I sought the Lord earnestly and prayed, "God, would You give us a church in the heart of this city, just for the lost, least, little, lonely and last?"

There is more to this story written in my first book. For now, I will leave you with this; when you pray, be willing to be the answer to your prayers. I am a testimony of just that, November of 2005; God used this little donkey to plant a church, just for people like the single moms at the tea.

They brought the little children to Him, Mark 10:13. As mentioned earlier, God moved us up "the hill" into a former funeral home. We were now able to do so much more for families and the little people. During our first summer in the new location, we launched the "Kid's Club" program, July through August every Monday, Wednesday, and Friday inner-city kids age 5-12 attended. Every day packed with activities, exciting Bible lessons, lots of fun, and food. Every Wednesday was community day. We invited our friends, guests from the city to speak with the kids. Among them, a police officer instructing about safety, health professional instructing about proper hygiene and a Jujitsu instructor teaching nonviolent self-protection.

We held a closing program at the end of the summer for parents to see what their children learned, ending with a cook-out and ice cream buffet with all the fixings for the entire family. During the summer outreach, we had the privilege of sharing God's love with over 50 kids. Later in this story, I share about one young man named Alex, who was among those impacted.

In 2009 God spoke to Tim, the director of "Uncharted Waters Sports Ministry." God made it clear to Tim that He wanted the ministry to offer their program for free to underserved inner-city kids. Their ministry, until that point, was for white and blue-collar churches that could afford their program. Hope Community Church scheduled UWSM for a week-long program at their church. Hope loves their city well and is a dear friend, and faithful supporter of Somebody Cares New England since 2006. They knew of the outreach we had done the previous summer and recommended us to be the recipient of UWSM generous offer.

We had a fantastic week, their team was incredible with the children, and their program was outstanding. The team loved being with us and thanked us for allowing them to come and serve. I was like, "Are you kidding? We are the ones who are thankful and more blessed by you coming." Then Tim said something to me that has stayed with me through the years. He said, "We go to churches all over the nation and other countries. We minister in some of the most financially well off churches.

But what we experienced here with you people on the hill has made a huge impact on my team."

He proceeded, "Often the kids that attend camp and our team are served sandwiches, chips, Kool-Aid, and cookies every day for meals. You served us a different menu every day of fresh, healthy food, prepared, and served with excellence. We bring little prizes like sweatbands from our ministry for the kids who memorize Scripture. You people provided every child with a brand new toy at the end of the program, they even got to pick out themselves. We saw you love kids in a tangible way that most churches talk about, but few do. How do you do it? You say you are an all-volunteer staff with no budget?" My reply to him was. "Oh, it's simple, we have a staff that loves God and loves people, and we always pray, "Lord, we will freely give whatever You give us, and You always give Your best." We have learned to FROG, which means *fully rely on God* for everything.

Sometimes God is so kind to let us know the impact we have, and we are careful to give all the glory to Him. Remember, I mentioned Alex? Well, Hope Community Church is a forerunner in New England serving in child advocacy within the Foster Care system. A member of Hope, and friend of Somebody Cares, Pam, is Alex's foster mother.

He was removed from his home here in Haverhill and placed in Pam's family for care. One day while sharing the Gospel with Alex, she invited him to receive the Lord. His response to her is the very reason we do what we do. Alex said, "I accepted the Lord at the Somebody Cares summer program last year." Pam thanked me for the work we do and encouraged us that although we may not have the opportunity to find out what the Lord does through us, to keep doing what we do, loving people to life! We know Alex is only one of the hundreds of children that God has reached with His love.

He sets the lonely in families, Psalm 68:6 (NLT). Her name was Barbara; she was a senior citizen that frequented our food pantry. She never took any groceries, though; she only wanted a bag of chips and a cup of coffee. She was all of 4'11 weighing in about 85 pounds, and one feisty, little Greek lady.

Serving the low income distressed population, we learn about the hardships they endure. It is no wonder why most people we serve hate life. The circumstances she lived in were less than desirable for anyone to be in.

She never married or had children, and she couldn't read or write. She lived with her deceased brother's son and his wife, sleeping on the couch in the living room on the third floor of a rundown apartment building with no air conditioning.

We always greeted little Barbara with enthusiasm and hugs, but she was a tough one to win over. Whenever she saw my car in the parking lot she would come to my office, stare in at me, banging on the window. I would let her in, give her chips and coffee, and listen to her as she would say the same thing over and over with absolute confidence. "You're going to get me out of hell." I always redirected her to God as the one who would rescue her and would offer to pray for her, but she let me know, in no uncertain terms, she was not interested.

Then one day, when I said, "Jesus is the one who saves us from hell, Barbara, would you like to know Him?" Her answer challenged me, "Oh, I know Him, and He told me you are going to get me out of hell!" God hadn't told me that! I thought to myself; you're a crafty one pulling the God card on me! I thought if God did tell her that, what was I supposed to do about it now?

As she continued to talk about the hell she lived in and that every day wanted to kill herself because she felt so hopeless. She knew she could never afford an apartment. Her social security check was only $530 a month, of which $250 a month went for rent. The rest went for chips, coffee, eating out, and cigarettes. We found out the reason she never took any groceries from the food pantry or bought any; it was because she wasn't allowed; there was no room in the refrigerator for anything she wanted.

In my head, I heard myself saying, no way, your calendar is already over the top busy, you can't do this, you don't have the time. Besides, I didn't have any housing resources. Ah, but little did I know, God had other plans. I prayed with her, "Lord, if you want to use this donkey, here I am, lead me!"

Sure enough, as Jehovah Jireh always does, He provided. Through relationships I have built in the city, I began to search out where to start the housing journey. I filled out her application for senior assisted housing. But Barbara didn't have, even one of the requirements to qualify her to move in. She had no doctor (to get physical), no picture ID (never had a license). She had no utility bill (to prove residence); she had no birth certificate (claiming to be born in the back of a pickup truck in Chicago), no school records (she never went to school), no bank account and no marriage certificate. There was no documentation found for this woman's life.

How can that be? How on earth did I get this assignment? I felt so incompetent and unqualified for this ridiculous, impossible situation. I couldn't turn in the application without even proof that this was who she claimed to be, although she had a social security and Medicare card, which could have been fake for all we knew.

But God is the way maker; He is the way where there seems to be no way. Miracle after miracle happened. He parted Barbara's Red Sea, and in less than two weeks, she was in her new sweet studio apartment. The first Sunday after we moved Barbara in, she started attending the church. Again, I asked her if she would like to know Jesus as her Lord and Savior; it was then that she prayed to receive Christ.

I gave her a picture she saw hanging on the wall at church that she liked. At one of our membership luncheons, we had everyone put their thumbprint on the family tree. Their colorful thumbprint filled the tree as if they were the leaves. I added hers to the picture and told her, "You have a Father that loves you, and He placed you in a family that loves you. He not only made a place for you in your new apartment, but He also made a place for you on the family tree." Her eyes filled with tears and twinkled as she said, "I told you, didn't I? I told you, you were going to get me out of hell!"

I would share all the incredible details of how the Lord worked in her life, but I would need another book. What I will tell you is what the director of senior housing said, "I don't know who you know or how you did it, but nobody, even with all the documentation required, gets in here in less than two months, let alone less than two weeks. And another thing, I just have to tell on God. I was concerned about how I was going to furnish the place, as money is always our challenge in this ministry. Besides, at the time, I was sixty-six years old, and the last thing I wanted to do was try to find a truck and haul furniture.

The director of senior housing called me to say, "Yesterday the man three doors down from Barbara's apartment passed away in the hospital. The family wants to donate to a non-profit that helps people. Are you able to use the entire contents of his apartment?" I joyfully thanked her while asking, "Do you think someone could help me move it three doors down?" She said, "Oh, we can take care of all that for you!" I joyfully accepted the offer, thinking to myself, "Of course you can!" I am continuously and joyfully amazed by Him!

The last shall be first, and the first shall be last. Luke 13:30. The First Nations People of America are, for the most part, the forgotten ones. I have never seen a report in the news of a Native American burning the American flag, blowing up a building, kneeling during the national anthem, or shooting up schools. Yet, these beautiful, honoring people have never used the injustice done against them as an excuse to be dishonorable and retaliate against the very ones who caused them such cruel, injustice. They are dear to the heart of God, as are all people, and He has not forgotten them!

It was the summer of 2004, when my daughter Bethany and I traveled to California sent on a mission trip designed by God. Only this mission trip wasn't to help others! The Lord had a mission, and it was something He planned just for us. Before going further, I want to give a little background that demonstrates just how intimate and intentional God is in the lives of His children.

It all started back in the fall of 2002, Pastor Charlie Sweet, an elder and prophet at Redeemer Church (then Mt. Zion), in Utica, NY., prophesied the word of the Lord to me and every word of it has come to pass. I only sharing three components that pertain to this testimony.

- The Lord was going to bless me with $1,000.00. It is not for the ministry, but it was for something He wanted me to do.

- He said that God was going to use me to preach the Gospel using the performing arts as He did through the ministry of Aimee Simple McPherson.

- The instruction was to go to the Los Angeles Dream Center. God wanted me to see it with my own eyes to enlarge my vision.

- He was going to establish a center through me in my city that even government officials would scratch their heads, wondering how we had accomplished it without government funding.

Well, sure enough, God used my dear friends Sandy and Dr. Gene Heacock, the founders of *Partners with Christ* and *House on the Rock*, to bless me with $1,000.00! They knew nothing of the prophetic word. When they handed me the check, they said, "The Lord has something for you to do, this is not for the ministry, this is for you. Immediately out of my mouth came, "I am going to the LA Dream Center, God is sending me out to spy the land!"

What an exciting ten days of divine appointments and prophetic fulfillment those days were. No words can capture and describe the blissful, hilarious joy one gets when they are dead center in the perfect will of God. I am doing my best to give only the highlights, although every moment of every day was full of miraculous, divine appointments.

We landed in LA and lodged on-site at the Dream Center for four nights. I was more than thrilled to be there. Several years earlier, I had read Matthew Barnett's book, "The Church that Never Sleeps." If you want to learn more about the center, it is a worthwhile read. They should put a warning on the front cover that reads, "This book has the potential to rock your world, turn it upside down and ruin your comfortable, cozy, carefree Christian life!" It was one of the books the Lord used in preparing me to serve as a prayer, compassion missionary. As I look back over the years, I am in awe of how the Lord has intricately weaved the men that mentored me, at the time not in person, but through their videos or books. I am in awe of how He then has brought them personally into my life, as they continue to impact me. Revelation 3:7 with the key of David He opens doors that no one can shut and shuts doors that no one can open.

God opened the door for me to have a personal appointment with Matthew Barnett. I knew he was the pastor of Angelus Temple, as well as director of the Dream Center, but did not know that I would be going to the church that Sunday. The

Center ran a shuttle bus transporting their residents to the church for service.

Aimee Simple McPherson was the founder of the Four Square denomination and the little lady that God used to miraculously build Angelus Temple in 1923. I felt as if I were dreaming and never wanted to wake up! There on the front row was Aimee's son Rolf, over eighty years old, the retired pastor still attending his mom's church. The church was famous for the miracles. Crutches, canes, braces, and other medical artifacts hung along the wall as a testimony of God's miracle-working power.

While in California, we hopped a puddle jumper (a mini plane) to Redding, California, to attend the 'Open Heavens' conference at Bethel Church. Through a Kingdom connection, Bethany and I were invited to lodge at a beautiful, privately owned horse ranch that had a little one-room house on the property, built just for prayer. Methinks to myself, "I must be in heaven, this little donkey is lodging at a multi-million-dollar horse ranch, with a house of prayer."

While at the conference, one of the resident prophets noticed on my name tag where I am from as he speaks, "I see you re-digging the wells of revival on the property of Bradford College campus. I see you with a little shovel, and you have been digging a long time, until now. You can go no further; you hit granite. You prop the shovel in the pile of dirt behind you. As you lean on it, you wipe your brow. I hear the Lord saying, "Daughter, I am right behind you with a bulldozer. Step aside, and I will breakthrough."

You know my eyes were popping out of the sockets, right? So crazy! If ever I doubted for a moment, the prophetic gift was for the church today; it is forever blown up! The testimony of Jesus is the Spirit of Prophecy (Rev. 19:10). God sees and knows everything!

The prophet went on, the Lord says, "He is going to use you in a Native American Resolution that will break open the entire region for revival." A Native American Resolution? What on earth is that? I had not a clue!

We continued praying on the former Bradford College campus for several years after that word, and God did what He said He would do (stay tuned for more). During this time, I was attending Community Christian Fellowship (CCF Ministries), in Lowell, Massachusetts. I never wanted to participate in a church outside of Haverhill, the city I was called to, but Father knows best! I had just returned from my California trip when my Pastor, Apostle Rafael Najem, asked me to preach Wednesday nights for a month to train the people as missionaries to their city.

It was then I shared about the call to a Native American Resolution. I was amazed as three intercessors about to fall off their seats onto the floor with shouts of joy and hilarious laughter. I was in shock and awe, as Apostle Najem came to the mic to explain. That same week I was in California receiving the word, Cindy Noon, the lead intercessor of CCF Lowell, told him the Lord had spoken to the intercessors in prayer that CCF was going to be a part of a reconciliation with Native Americans.

From 2004 to 2006, we all prayed, as we continued seeking God. We prayed asking the Lord how, when, and where this resolution was going to happen. It wasn't until sometime later I found out why it took so long.

I talked with Lou Engle, the visionary, founder, and mobilizer of the prophetic prayer gatherings known as 'The Call.' Lou advised me to contact Dr. Negiel Bigpond and gave me his cell phone number. Dr. Bigpond had been to the White House for a meeting with President Bush regarding a resolution between the Native Americans and the United States Federal Government.

Was this really happening? I called Dr. Bigpond, explained my prophetic word, and about the what intercessors in Lowell had received. I said to him, "I am just a little old' white lady from Haverhill, a little donkey, I have no clue what I do!" He proceeded to tell me all the components needed for the resolution to take place.

The following are only a few he mentioned. A State Senator was needed to have the resolution drawn up and signed by Congress, then presented to an indigenous, pure-blooded, Native American born in the region (none of which I even remotely knew of).

Little did I know that Senator Steven Pangiotakos was an active member of CCF Ministries in Lowell and was more than willing to take on the assignment. Now I just needed an indigenous Native American to join in the fun.

So, one ordinary day, I turned the corner of my street, and there standing in full color is a Native American. A feather in his braid, his arms crossed, watching the sunset. What? On my street? Oh, my goodness, now what do I do? I can't see myself knocking on his front door telling him this wild and crazy story and expect him to 'come out and play' with us. Over a year, I looked at his house from the window. I prayed repeatedly, "Lord, I am not doing anything without Your leading." And then one day it happened, I drove around the corner of my street and he was gone! Packed up and gone! To where I had no clue, I didn't even know what his name was. My heart was heavy, I felt like I failed the Lord.

But God had a perfect plan. The short version is, my mom called from Florida and asked me to pack up her house and bring her to live with me. She had taken a fall and was afraid to live alone anymore. After moving her into my home, I called Elder Services to come and set her up with services she needed. Then it happened! God's divine destiny at work again! There were two women, one just starting the job that day and the other, her last day before retiring. They were sitting in my house, at my kitchen table. The soon to retire woman said, "I used to live right across the street from you on the corner." Wide-eyed and mystified, I said, "Are you married to a Native American?" She answered, "Why yes, his birth name is Sly Fox. When a white Catholic family adopted him, they changed his name to John Oakley."

Somebody pinch me, was this happening? I was not going to miss this divine moment! I enthusiastically asked, "Do you think your husband would meet with me to discuss a Native American Resolution of Apology?" She joyfully responded, "Of course, I am sure he would be happy to." Meet we did, although he was skeptical, that Congress would agree to it. He said, "I will believe it when I see it." Even though doubting, he was willing to commit to being an intricate part of making it all happen.

Out of my mind with joy, I called Dr. Bigpond and told him all God had done. We set the date, September 23, 2006. He was so kind to come to lead us in the Resolution at CCF Lowell. My new, full-blooded, Mashpee Wampanoag friend Sly Fox brought several of his Native friends to see and hear the apology for themselves. It was so surreal to be a part of this historic day. I learned later that the John Eliot Church in Lowell, Massachusetts, was in honor of John as our nation's first missionary to the Native Americans. God chose Lowell, Massachusetts, and as always, lines up every vital detail, He thinks of everything! Following is the article from the Lowell Sun 9/30/2006.

LOWELL -- Dr. Negiel Bigpond was presented with the formal Resolution of Apology from the Commonwealth of Massachusetts for the Native American people during a ceremony at the Community Christian Fellowship in Lowell last Sunday.

The night began with a few words and a prayer by Pastor Raffoul Najem of CCF, and then God Bless America was sung by church member Asheley Clark.

Bethany Yeo, the director of the Justice House of Prayer in Boston, was present for the event and offered a powerful prayer for the safety of our nation.

Pastor Najem reminisced about Dr. Bigpond's last visit to CCF, where he offered Dr. Bigpond a verbal apology for the injustices inflicted upon the Native Americans in the name of God and displayed his servanthood by washing Dr. Bigpond's feet in the manner that Jesus did with his disciples' feet according to the Bible.

Dr. Bigpond gave Pastor Najem a Native American nickname, "Strong Wings." Senator Steven Panagiotakos, who initiated the formal apology from the state, was also present.

"It's always nice when I come here. It feels like home," he said.

Panagiotakos proceeded to read the Resolution of Apology and presented it to Dr. Bigpond and fellow Native American Sly Fox (John Oakley).

Dr. Bigpond then spoke to the congregation, "I see warriors in this room," he said. He encouraged the people to keep fighting for what they believe in and to make their voices be heard. He also encouraged unity between all ethnic groups.

Dr. Bigpond spoke of hope for the future of the Native American people. "I want America to recognize my grandchildren. One day they'll be proud to say 'I'm an Indian.' They won't be ashamed," Dr. Bigpond said. "To a native heart, justice is the picture of a river that never stops moving."

He then made a promise that the people would see changes in government, tribes, nations, families and more in 30 days.

The night ended with a heartwarming song by Dr. Bigpond in his native language. The words of the song mean "always look forward, never look back." The congregation joined him in this song of hope for the future.

"Tonight, history was made as a Massachusetts Senate Resolution of Apology was presented to Dr. Negiel Bigpond," said Pastor Najem. "We thank God for opening this door and we pray that the Senate and House of Representatives will support the resolution so that the progress that has been made toward reconciliation and healing continues."

The Lord will vindicate His people in the face of those who stole and ravished their land. It is a humbling privilege to serve the Lord in prayer and prophetic acts as He restores the dignity of His people. He has not forgotten the injustice done against them in their homeland by white men. God forgive us and heal our land!

Although it is not clear, I wanted to include an electronic copy of the historic 'Resolution of Apology' document signed by legislators apologizing for the injustice done against the Native Americans here in Massachusetts.

The Massachusetts State Senate

Resolutions

MEMORIALIZING THE CONGRESS OF THE UNITED STATES TO PASS SENATE JOINT
RESOLUTION 15 APOLOGIZING TO ALL NATIVE AMERICAN PEOPLES
ON BEHALF OF THE UNITED STATES.

WHEREAS, THROUGHOUT HISTORY, THE COMMONWEALTH OF MASSACHUSETTS HAS BEEN INSTRUMENTAL IN THE STRUGGLE TO ESTABLISH DEMOCRACY AND SECURE THE RIGHTS AND LIBERTIES OF AMERICANS; AND

WHEREAS, THE DECLARATION OF RIGHTS OF THE COMMONWEALTH OF MASSACHUSETTS WAS THE FIRST ENUMERATION OF CIVIL RIGHTS AND LIBERTIES BY AMERICANS, WHICH SERVED AS A MODEL FOR THE UNITED STATES CONSTITUTION AND BILL OF RIGHTS; AND

WHEREAS, THE COMMONWEALTH OF MASSACHUSETTS HAS A RICH NATIVE AMERICAN HISTORY WITH INDIGENOUS TRIBES SUCH AS MASSACHUSET FROM SUFFOLK COUNTY, THE NIPMUC FROM CENTRAL MASSACHUSETTS, THE STOCKBRIDGE FROM BERKSHIRE COUNTY AND THE WAMPANOAG FROM CAPE COD AND THE ISLANDS; AND

WHEREAS, THE COMMONWEALTH OF MASSACHUSETTS ACKNOWLEDGES THE LONG HISTORY OF OFFICIAL DEPREDATIONS AND ILL-CONCEIVED POLICIES BY THE UNITED STATES GOVERNMENT REGARDING NATIVE AMERICAN TRIBES AND BELIEVES THAT THE CONGRESS OF THE UNITED STATES SHOULD OFFER AN APOLOGY TO ALL NATIVE PEOPLES ON BEHALF OF THE UNITED STATES; AND

WHEREAS, THE ANCESTORS OF TODAY'S NATIVE PEOPLES HAVE INHABITED THE LAND OF THE PRESENT-DAY UNITED STATES SINCE TIME IMMEMORIAL AND FOR THOUSANDS OF YEARS BEFORE THE ARRIVAL OF PEOPLES OF EUROPEAN ORIGIN; AND

WHEREAS, THE NATIVE PEOPLES HAVE FOR MILLENNIA HONORED, PROTECTED AND STEWARDED THIS LAND THAT WE CHERISH; AND

WHEREAS, THE UNITED STATES GOVERNMENT HAS VIOLATED MANY OF THE TREATIES RATIFIED BY CONGRESS AND OTHER DIPLOMATIC AGREEMENTS WITH NATIVE AMERICAN TRIBES; AND

WHEREAS, DESPITE CONTINUING MALTREATMENT OF NATIVE PEOPLES BY THE UNITED STATES, THE NATIVE PEOPLES HAVE REMAINED COMMITTED TO THE PROTECTION OF THIS GREAT LAND, AS EVIDENCED BY THE FACT THAT, ON A PER CAPITA BASIS, MORE NATIVE PEOPLE HAVE SERVED IN THE UNITED STATES ARMED FORCES AND PLACED THEMSELVES IN HARM'S WAY IN DEFENSE OF THE UNITED STATES IN EVERY MAJOR MILITARY CONFLICT THAN ANY OTHER ETHNIC GROUP; AND

WHEREAS, NATIVE PEOPLES ARE ENDOWED BY THEIR CREATOR WITH CERTAIN UNALIENABLE RIGHTS, AND THAT AMONG THOSE ARE LIFE, LIBERTY, AND THE PURSUIT OF HAPPINESS; NOW THEREFORE BE IT

RESOLVED, THAT THE MASSACHUSETTS SENATE HEREBY URGES THE SENATE AND HOUSE OF REPRESENTATIVES OF THE UNITED STATES TO PASS, PENDING SENATE JOINT RESOLUTION 15, APOLOGIZING TO ALL NATIVE AMERICAN PEOPLES ON BEHALF OF THE UNITED STATES OF AMERICA; AND BE IT FURTHER

RESOLVED, THAT A COPY OF THESE RESOLUTIONS BE FORWARDED BY THE CLERK OF THE SENATE TO THE CLERKS OF THE SENATE AND HOUSE OF REPRESENTATIVES OF THE UNITED STATES.

SENATE: ADOPTED, JUNE 22, 2006.

PRESIDENT OF THE SENATE

CLERK OF THE SENATE

OFFERED BY:

SENATOR STEVEN C. PANAGIOTAKOS

SENATOR EDWARD M. AUGUSTUS, JR.

SENATOR STEVEN A. BADDOUR

SENATOR HARRIETTE L. CHANDLER

SENATOR SUSAN FARGO

SENATOR THERESE MURRAY

SENATOR ROBERT O'LEARY

SENATOR STANLEY C. ROSENBERG

SENATOR DIANNE WILKERSON

182

Chapter 9

Destiny Revealed Through History

P rayer and intercession will often lead us to the people, places, and nations that one has prayed. It was while living in Kingston, New Hampshire, before the Lord sent me to Haverhill, that I watched the first transformation video. It was then I experienced travailing intercession. The word travail is interchangeable with labor.

Just like in natural delivery, it takes place after you have carried something in your heart for the fullness of time and comes on you suddenly. The following verses reference the word labor and zeal regarding prayer. Colossians 4:12-13 *Epaphras, who is one of you, a bondservant of Christ, greets you, always laboring fervently for you in prayers, that you may stand perfect and complete in all the will of God. 13 For I bear him witness that he has a great zeal for you, and those who are in Laodicea, and those in Hierapolis.* Galatians 4:19 *"My little children, for whom I labor in birth again until Christ is formed in you."*

The prayer of travailing intercession is God desiring to create an opening to bring forth a measure of life. If the opportunity were already in place, there would not be a need for travail. Just as the opening of the natural womb is enlarged to bring forth the baby, so travail creates an opening or way. With travail, there is always a way opened for life, newness, change, and increase. Travail is a form of intense intercession given by the Holy Spirit to those who will avail themselves to travail in prayer. Once His promise is brought forth, there is great joy and relief when the delivery is over!

It was Lou Engle who I first heard say, 'History is His Story,' which I found to be so accurate as we researched the history of Haverhill. The handiwork of God, Master Weaver, was making a beautiful needlepoint picture story for us to understand how and what to pray into the destiny of our city.

My friend Margret Foley, born and raised in Haverhill, has been clipping and saving articles from the local newspapers for decades. It wasn't until 2000 did she understand why she had the three-ring binder full of Haverhill's history. I was so excited the day she showed me the many years of her work. We would go to the Haverhill Public Library and pour over the fascinating details of history. Being that the library is to be a quiet place, it was difficult containing our joyful enthusiasm as layer upon layer of information gave insight for us to pray onsite. If you know Peggy, you know how difficult it is to contain ones' enthusiasm when with her! She is, in every good sense of the word, 'a hoot' and so much fun. Peggy writes the following as she tells how the Lord led her to research.

In the late 80's I discovered a book called "Taking Our Cities for God, (How to Break Spiritual Strongholds)," by John Dawson.

184

While reading this book, God opened my eyes and heart. It changed my life forever, and from then on, I looked at towns/cities from God's perspective. So there I was using both Scripture and Dawson's book to map out the land. So exciting, I felt like a detective! Not long after reading that book, our local newspaper printed information on every neighborhood. It was then I began a long journey of gathering information about my city.

The next book God led me to was "Healing America's Wounds," also by John Dawson. This book so gripped my heart that it was my first "real" experience with intercession for the land, for both the Native Americans and the African Americans. I was heartbroken; I never thought I would recover from all these injustices. It felt like all these injustices were all my fault.

The Lord was allowing me the heartbreak and pain of the injustice through intercession. Back then, I didn't have a name for it, all I knew was, I couldn't stop crying while praying. My heart ached. So much so, that I thought, is this deep sorrow how I will live the rest of my life. In one sense, it is partly true because once the Holy Spirit touches you so profoundly, you can never go back to what life used to be, you are forever changed. The good news is as we partner with God to intercede He does lift the intense feeling of pain as we pray for healing and restoration.

My heart knew it was the work of the Holy Spirit praying through me, but my natural mind thought, what could I do about the past?

The Bible is full of Scriptures regarding God's heart for the land. Numbers 13-14 prayer walking, spying out the land, Joshua 1:1-9 re-digging the wells and claiming the land; Nehemiah 1-6 having a heart for our cities and towns; and Exodus 23:20-33 "See, I am sending an angel ahead of you to guard you along the way and to bring you back to the place I have prepared." You see, if we pay close attention to God, He has already mapped everything out for us.

O my goodness, it was all coming together – God is interested in our land and restoring it. I was becoming a repairer of the breach between God and His land. After all, wasn't it He who created the earth and had a perfect plan and destiny for His land? Isn't that what Psalm 24 says? I realized that the land is all about people. They are intertwined, you can't have one without the other. All injustice comes from people, so as the nation's healed, so are the people. How great is that? It's like a two for one special!

Ok, I was now starting to get it! It was now time to battle for the land and bring down the strongholds - there was no turning back. Of course, I didn't do this alone. There were a few of us that came together to "make a plan."

We were learning to pay attention and listen to the Holy Spirit and began to hear and see what He wanted to show us. It was a lot like a puzzle. There were tons of pieces that somehow needed fitting into the makeup of our city. I began to realize that cities and towns are the mind and heart of the nation. I started to compile a list of all my questions.

We were after the injustices which became the strongholds in our city. Who were our forefathers, what kind of covenants did they make? We needed to re-dig the wells, another book God used on my journey, "Re-Digging the Wells of Revival" by Lou Engle.

I get so excited when I think back on the days, which seemed so long ago. Because of all the prayer walks, fasting, worship, and intercession, we were able to see our city the way God does and watch Him restore so many things. He is our Amazing King who can't wait to bring healing to His land, and He wants us to partner with Him. How can we not say yes?

Jeremiah 29:11 reveals God's heart and plan for people and lands. "For I know the plans I have for you," declares the LORD, "plans to prosper you and not to harm you, plans to give you hope and a future."

The question we have to ask ourselves is, "Do I have the faith to believe God wants to restore the land and the people?" And will the answer be, "Yes Lord, I want to be a part of Your plan."

What we discovered when we started the prayer journey in 1999 would take volumes, in this chapter I am only going to focus on one of the many exciting testimonies of healing of the land. We discovered the first statue erected in America, giving tribute to a woman was in honor of Hannah Duston. The statue is located in the heart of the city in the Grand Army Republic Park diagonal from City Hall. We extrapolated the following information from haverhillusa.com.

Hannah Duston (1657-1732) is noted in history for her daring escape from ten Native Americans. On March 15, 1697, Hannah, her 1-week old daughter Martha, and others were kidnapped and forced to walk over forty-five miles in the dead of winter to a site along the Merrimack River near Concord, NH. History records her baby was thrown against a tree and murdered because she was crying inconsolably, and the Natives were afraid of being caught. Soon after her baby's murder, Hannah learned they were taking her to a faraway village. Fearing for her own life, Hannah plotted her escape knowing that there would be little chance of any rescue attempt being made to save her.

On March 31, 1697, the young warriors of the encampment left Hannah with two senior men of the tribe, several women and children. Hannah saw this as an opportunity for her escape once everyone was asleep. She fled for her life but decided to go back to kill and scalp them to prove her story and collect the bounty.

Hannah story was revived again in the 1800s during the era of "Manifest Destiny" by writers such as Henry David Thoreau and John Greenleaf Whittier, who were looking to tell the stories of American heroes and heroines. But as the original Cotton Mather version of the story was rewritten and retold, people changed the narrative to suit their purposes—often omitting the part of the story in which she killed the two older men, women, and sleeping children. Her statue erected in 1879.

In the fall of 2015, I came across a YouTube video of a little 11-year old Native American girl named Mishayle, giving her testimony at Dr. Jay Swallow's church. Following her testimony, she prayed for Dr. Jay Swallow, his wife, and the church members.

Mishayle was born with a fatal disease that crippled and eventually took her life at age ten. As her mother sat weeping at her bedside, she prayed for God to give back her daughter's life, not diseased as she was before her death, but for Mishayle to be healed and whole.

Jesus brought Mishayle to heaven. In His presence, there is no sickness, no disease, and no infirmity. The Lord healed her as her mom was talking to the Lord. He told Mishayle she needed to return to tell others about His healing love. God is using her powerful testimony to bring healing and deliverance to His people. I have included the link if you would like to see and hear it for yourself,
https://www.youtube.com/watch?v=oVYZmLZb8j8.

In the background, there is a song that gripped my heart. For months I searched diligently but could not find any information about this song. Through the anointing, the Lord was doing something supernatural in my heart. My experience with the Holy Spirit as I listened and prayed was like when I watched the transformation video in 1999, I knew it was supernatural. Every day for several weeks, I felt compelled to listen. Every time my heart stirred with travailing intercession for the Native people. I knew God was using this song to draw my heart for His kingdom purpose once again!

Then one Wednesday night, while praying with a few Northpoint students just before Thanksgiving break, I was led by the Holy Spirit to bring the video so they too could join in prayer with me for the Native Americans. I shared with the students that I had recently learned that many Natives did not participate in our 'Thanksgiving traditions.' It is not a time of celebration but of mourning the loss of freedom and their homeland. I played the song as we worshiped, waiting for the Holy Spirit's leading to pray. It happened, the same anointing (presence of God) I experienced at home occurred while we were together that night.

As I wept and interceded for the Lord to restore the Native people and their land, out of my mouth, the Holy Spirit spoke prophetically. If someone that didn't understand intercession were present, they would have been alarmed by the intense passion as these words came from the Lord through my mouth, "I have not forgotten My people, I have not forgotten them! They are My people, and I am their God. I will heal and restore them, and I will make known My love for them."

I knew I stepped into prophetic destiny. God was up to something good, as always. I responded with a burning heart of love for the people of this land, "Here I am Lord, send me, use me according to Your Word." Up until that time, the ministry of Somebody Cares New England was mostly involved with New England. But that night, God put it in my heart to offer whatever resources we had to demonstrate His love to my brothers and sisters on any reservation that there was an open door.

I began reaching out to my Kingdom relationships throughout New England. I was searching for the right connection offering to come to serve and be a blessing with our resources. For months I reached out with phone calls and emails. We just wanted to help these beautiful people, give away a tractor-trailer truck of goods for free and throw a block party with all the works. We were offering to host it, bring the volunteers, raise funds for it, and no one responded.

One day while talking to my friend, Linda Clark. I told her; I cannot find a venue to be a blessing. I have hit a dead end. Linda is involved with several prophetic ministries that facilitate prophetic acts of intercession for the healing of the land. She told me the Native people are very reserved; they do not trust the motives of white people; you think? Is it any wonder? Linda asked if I had reached out to Dr. Bigpond as a well-respected Chief of the Euchee (Yuchi) Tribe. She thought maybe he could connect me with someone in New England to vouch for us that we had no ulterior motives, no hidden agenda, we just wanted to be a blessing.

I called my friend Dr. Bigpond, who lives in Oklahoma. Remember, he was the one that led us in the Resolution of Apology. I told him what the Lord had spoken through intercession and that my heart was bursting to be a blessing. I told him of my efforts to find a venue in New England. We just wanted to demonstrate the love of the Father to our brothers and sisters.

I said, "Dr. Bigpond, you have trusted Kingdom relationships across this land. Is there anyone you know in New England that you could talk to and let them know what we are offering for free? We just want to be a blessing." He said he was in a meeting at that very moment with First and Second Chief of the Muscogee Creek Nation and Tribal Chiefs from across America. He had stepped outside the meeting to take my call.

I apologized for interrupting such an important meeting and shocked that he would exit the meeting to take my call. His response was both humbling and honoring, "I answered because it's my friend, the warrior, Marlene Yeo." He said he would bring up our offer during the meeting and see if there was an open door.

Shortly after, he called back and said, "I have an open door for you!" I was so excited and asked, "Awesome, where?" In his calm, gentle manner, he said, "We all agreed you need to come here to Oklahoma with your blessing. Our people are in great distress. Suicide is taking the lives of our young. Our elders are sickly because of poor nutrition. We need you here."

My frightening thoughts were, no way! I can't do that! How will I ever get all my stuff there? You know, the stuff in Luke 10 that Jesus told the disciples not to take with them! In my rendition, I am sending you into every city I will go, only don't take any stuff! After all, I had a container full of stuff; grills, canopies, tables, chairs, a bounce house, and all the other stuff needed for a block party. Besides stuff, there were over a hundred volunteers who had served over the years, who knew what to do; they were all here in the greater Haverhill area! But God spoke to my heart in that millisecond, "You asked for an open door, here it is!" So without spewing all my doubts and fears, out jumps from my mouth, "Excellent, when do you want us to come?"

After I hung up, I thought to myself, and who is this *us* I mentioned. Besides me, myself and I, Father, Son, and Holy Spirit at that time, there was no one else. It was a set up for another Kingdom adventure! Once again, I needed reminding what men say is impossible is not impossible for God. I was about to walk out over my head once again to see God's miraculous power at work.

And bless, we did! That year five prayer, compassion missionaries from Haverhill Massachusetts went to Okmulgee,

Oklahoma, on an exciting missions trip. If I were to write every detail of God's over the top, outrageous provision, it would take pages. What I will say is, WOW! I never dreamed it would be such a supernatural divine appointment for not only the ones we served but for us as well. We were invited by the Muscogee Creek Nation heads of Government to meet at their official government offices. We brought a gift basket to honor them and thank them for allowing us to come and serve. The Second Chief (liken to our Vice President of America) asked, "What brings you to our land?" Holding back the tears, I said, "While in prayer I heard the Spirit say, I have not forgotten my people, I am here to remind you, you are His beloved people, and He has not forgotten you!"

While in Oklahoma, I told Dr. Bigpond about the prophetic song that impacted me. He responded, "Oh, that's Andy Leong; he is the worship leader at 'Church on the Rock,' John Benefiel's church, here in Oklahoma. God was connecting the dots.

Here we were, at that moment in Oklahoma, while serving the First Nations people that God was so kind to let me know about this powerful song that He used to draw my heart into intercession for His beloved people. On our website www.somebodycaresne.org, there is a short video of our first missions trip with the song, used by permission, "You are our God (Ma'heo' o)" from the album "Dream God's Dreams", Church on the Rock 2009.

When I testify of what God did on that trip, those five days with us five little donkeys, it brings me to tears, and I find myself lost for the words to tell of His glorious deeds. On the last day of that trip while saying our goodbyes to the people, we grew to know and love, Dr. Bigpond said, "See you all next year, we look forward to having you again." I don't remember thinking or saying we were coming back. But in my heart, I knew it was so, and so it was.

November of 2017, we returned, this time there were nine little donkeys. Among them was my dear friend from high school, Janice (Atwood) Surette. God used Janice to witness to me in 1976 about the love of Jesus and her salvation experience. I know her prayers were instrumental in bringing me to the Lord in January 1977. I also had the joy of my 12-year-old grandson Ayden serve with me.

November 2017 Second mission trip Okmulgee, Oklahoma

Front row left to right: Merrick Finn, Kathy Munro, Sandy Furtado, Marlene Yeo, Second Chief Louis Hicks, Principal Chief James Floyd, Ayden Yeo, Janice Surette, Paula Welch and Dr.

Bigpond's administrator, Kami Rush. Second row: Christopher Daigle and Christian Reynoso.

This second-year trip was beyond our wildest dreams. God had something so special it blew our minds. We meet with both the First and Second Chief, along with their staff and news reporters. As we sat there in the governmental oval office, First Chief asked, "Why is it that you come here now a second time and do for our people what you do?" It was in that prophetic moment I realized this was not only about all the beautiful things that the Lord was doing for the people we were serving; it was a part of my prophetic destiny.

We went unrehearsed, and without foreknowledge of what was about to happen, I said with tears, "Chief, there has been grave injustice done against your people by the white man. My ancestors, John and Priscilla Alden, were among those on the Mayflower that landed in Plymouth. I am here asking forgiveness on behalf of my ancestors and my city. The city I come from, Haverhill, Massachusetts, raised the first statue in America to honor a white woman, Hannah Dustin, from Haverhill. There is more to this story, but this lady has a hatchet raised in her hand, signifying her brutal violent act of scalping innocent Native women and children. I am ashamed that my city calls this a heroic act. Here today at this table sits my friend Janice, a direct descendent of Hannah Dustin. We are here to humbly ask forgiveness for the grave injustice done on behalf of our ancestors."

To my surprise, with tears in his eyes, he responded. "There was grave injustice we also did against the white man and even our brother against brother. Today neither you or I would do such things. I, too, ask forgiveness on behalf of my ancestors and give forgiveness to you and yours." Everyone there witnessed this was a holy moment that words cannot possibly convey.

At that Saturday's block party, we again blessed the people with a tractor-trailer of goods, music, cookout, and all the works. But the eternal purpose for us being there was to present the Gospel with signs and wonders. For the second year in a row, a powerful testimony and salvation message delivered by my very dear friend, JJ Ramirez, founder and director of Save Our Streets Ministries in Brazos Valley, TX.

That year, Second Chief took his hat off, bowed his head and prayed while JJ led the people in a prayer to receive Christ. Jay had a word of knowledge that there was someone with pain in their knee and that God wanted to heal them. It was the Chief. God healed him, and the Chief even testified!

Going back as I previously wrote, Dr. Bigpond came to Lowell, Massachusetts, to lead the Massachusetts Resolution of Apology. While he was here, I so wanted to bring him to Haverhill and have him pray with us to bless our city, but it was not part of God's plan at that time. The following are several components that needed to be set in place before that could happen.

God had used my connection with Dr. Bigpond and was about to do it again for the third time. Northpoint Bible College was the location chosen for the Assemblies of God "Awake, Awake," National Native American Convocation (Isaiah 51:9). Native leaders, pastors, and missionaries came from across North

America and Canada for a time of prayer and inspirational Native-led worship to God from the many Native tribes. For more information, see http://agnaf.com.

This Convocation was in response to the prophetic word given, "The Native American is a sleeping giant. He is awakening. The original Americans could become the evangelists who will help win America for Christ", (Billy Graham 1975 to Tom Huron Claus CHIEF Ministries).

Pastor Brent, whose church was here in this region, was responsible for organizing the event. He was the son of the Assemblies of God National Overseer of all the Native AG churches in America. Pastor Brent found an old sticky note in the back of a desk drawer that had my number that read, Marlene Yeo, has a heart to serve the Native Americans. Pastor Brent called and said, "I have no idea how this sticky note got here, but I was wondering if you would like to help serve this event we are planning to host here on the campus?"

I told him how several years before I had called his church in hopes of offering the resources we had to be a blessing to a New England Reservation. The person on the other end thanked me for calling and said, "Pastor Brent is a very busy man, I am not sure he will be able to return your call, but I will give him your message." When I told Brent, he apologized. It was his Associate Pastor who was no longer with him that wrote the note.

I assured him no apology was necessary and that there was a reason the Lord didn't open the door at that time. He wanted me to go to Oklahoma instead. I told him all about Dr. Bigpond and the 2006 Native American Resolution that he led us in. He was very interested in meeting Dr. Bigpond and wanted me to invite him to read the Resolution at the Convocation. Being a Kingdom networker, I knew this was another Kingdom assignment. My heart leaped with joy; now is the time for us here in Haverhill to fulfill our prophetic destiny; it's time to heal our land! Dr. Bigpond graciously accepted the invitation.

Friday night opening session Resolution of Apology. Pastor Brent (left), Dr. Bigpond (middle) and Apostle Najem (right). There was more that God wanted to do while Dr. Bigpond was here in Haverhill.

We had prayed and had known in our heart that now is the time for healing the land. Dr. Bigpond preached Sunday morning at our church, Community Christian Fellowship (CCF Haverhill).

He gave a prophetic message, "Now is the Time to Cross the Jordan; it's time to cross over the river into the promised land." (stay tuned to more on that).

That prophetic weekend, I also invited my dear Kingdom friends, Pastor Cindy Wermuth from Joplin, Missouri, along with her daughter-in-law Elisabeth, her son Daniel Wermuth III and Todd, another member of their prophetic team. They led worship and intercession both services Sunday morning. Sunday night, we had a prophetic gathering and invited Apostle Linda Clark to preach. Her message was titled, "Prophetic intercession that brings healing to the Land."

God is very strategic; there needed to be specific key people who understood what healing the land was. Those present for this historical time were key people in their area of the country that were involved with similar prophetic acts. It takes the right people, at the right time, for the right reasons, doing the right thing for the Lord to bring forth righteousness. Pastor Cindy's father was full-blooded Choctaw and the prophetic worship team that traveled from Washington State carried the anointing of prophetic intercession for the Native Americans. They ministered with Native drums, flutes, and many other instruments creating native sounds.

There were three locations we prayer walked in our city. Each site John Furtado blew the Shofar, and we boldly prayed, declaring and decreeing healing of the land. First on the list was the Hannah Dustin statue. There we did a prophetic act of forgiveness between a Native American, Pastor Cindy, and another descendent of Hannah Dustin, Martha Temple. Martha lives in Kingston, NH, on Great Pond. One of New Hampshire's most historic Native American paths is the southern trail, which led from Haverhill (Pentucket) to Massapaug known as Great Pond in Kingston NH. The trail from Kingston to Haverhill was known as "the place of the arrows." The location where the Native Americans discovered the stones used for the points of arrows. It is prevalent today to see the symbol of two arrows on art and clothing. Dr. Bigpond taught us, whenever you see the arrows, it means, "Always go forward, never go back."

The second location was the steps of City Hall. John blew the Shofar, we raised our voice and declared Jesus is the King of the hill, Haverhill. We decreed His rightful place is seated in the highest-ranking of government to rule and reign over our city, with righteousness and truth. (Isaiah 9:6)

The third location was over the Merrimack River. Now that we had broken the curses of injustice, we all raised our voices declaring the Kingdom has come and His will done in Haverhill, the city of God! There were about thirty people who joined us for that powerful, prophetic prayer walk. After finishing, we began our journey walking back to our cars at GAR Park.

The police pulled up next to us, asking what we were doing. I had the honor of answering, "We came here to pray and bless our city! Every act of kindness, every prayer we have ever prayed over our city, has been, "Lord bless this city and may your Kingdom destiny for this city be fulfilled and may we see it come to pass in our generation!"

John Furtado on the Basiliere Bridge, blowing the shofar over the city. This bridge connects the Bradford annex and Haverhill, June 3, 2018, "Healing the land."

Another testimony regarding the opening paragraphs of this chapter that prayer, and intercession often will lead us to the people, places, and nations that we lift in prayer. In our research, we learned that the Manifest Destiny was a phrase coined in 1845, that expressed the philosophy that drove the 19th-century U.S. territorial expansion. Manifest Destiny held that the United States was destined—by God, its advocates believed—to expand its dominion and spread democracy and capitalism across the entire North American continent, by driving out the Natives of the land.

Here we were, the least likely, little donkeys to be chosen for such a Kingdom assignment. To partner with God breaking off curses of the Manifest Destiny and declaring His manifest destiny, that the government of our Lord Jesus Christ shall rule and reign forever and ever Amen! And that He, the Lord, with righteous judgment, would come to bring justice on behalf of the First Nations people.

In closing, I share what Dr. Bigpond's mother told him before her passing, "You are like a river that gives me life, and without you, I cannot exist." It means that the next generation proves that we existed before them. Here in Haverhill, Massachusetts, the City of God, we experienced together the life-giving power of Kingdom relationships, making themselves available for Kingdom purposes. Revival rivers of God are flowing in our veins and out to our streets! May those yet to be born on the earth benefit from the previous generation because we fought the good fight and won. May they carry on in faith and obedience into the purpose of God for their generation!

Chapter 10

Donkeys Warn of Impending Danger

There are several reasons a donkey brays with a loud 'hee-haw' sound. They may be lonely, calling for a friend, excited about something, or anticipate their next meal. But this chapter title is chosen for this reason alone; they bray when they hear something that may pose a threat. In some countries, donkeys are put with the sheep to warn the owner of a predator.

Before I begin a little background. The Lord has often used the sheep analogy to train me as an under-shepherd under the tutelage of the Good Shepherd. Throughout the Bible, the Lord uses sheep and shepherd parables to help us better understand His relationship with His people. We learn so much about ourselves and God from the beautiful picture of His love and care for us. I liken these characteristics between sheep and the church as follows.

- Sheep: Are a flock animal that likes to be in a herd to graze together. They feel safest in a group; it is one of the ways they protect themselves from predators.

- Church: You can see this clearly, especially when Christians are in public. They are similar to sheep in that they are called 'groupies'; they are more comfortable interacting with their kind.

- Sheep: Certain breeds tend to stick together, even when they are placed in a mixed herd.

- Church: So true, we have the white church, black church, Hispanic church, and spiritually we have the liberal church, religious church, and conservative church. That is because 'deep calls unto deep' or the more familiar saying,' birds of a feather' flock together.

- Sheep: When one sheep decides to go somewhere the others will follow, whether it be a good or bad idea.

- Church: We see it all the time when one person is dissatisfied or offended; they share their concerns, sooner or later, as they slip out the back door, taking the others they influenced with them. One thing common in every type of church is, sheep have a strong instinct to follow other sheep with the same mindsets.

- Sheep: Often, butt each other over everything; it's the way they communicate.

- Church: I have experienced the not so joyous head butt. It usually follows a sermon or a meeting when something was said that exposed an area that needs healing in their soul.

- -Sheep: If one is hitting too hard and appears a threat to the others, you might want to isolate the head butt-er.

- Church: I have had a very unpleasant job of having to invite someone to leave the church, which is one of the unpleasant things about pastoring.

- Rams: Male sheep, use head butting to build up their strength and to establish the hierarchy within the herd.

- Church: A few of the brothers and I have butt heads.

The authority entrusted to me to serve as a pastor, both by God and my covering, has more than once been butt by the ones who say, "But(t) women can't lead!" To them, I always joyfully answer, "And you are so right! Right, in that, women *can't* lead men in their manhood or lead men in their role as a son, a brother, a husband, or as fathers. But(t) women can and do lead well as an example of submission to the Lord as head and as obedient disciples of Christ in teaching the biblical truths of the faith. It is those women; he calls and qualifies as teachers, pastors, prophets, evangelists, and yes, even church planters, better known as apostles (Romans 16:7).

The evidence surrounding my ministry is living proof of God's call on my life. I am so grateful to the Holy Spirit for the work He does in us so that He can do a work through us. As a pastor, I often must do things I dislike, and even at times have said, 'I hate.' One of those things I have a responsibility to do is warn someone of impending danger. It was not my personality profile to stand up or to speak up about anything! My first and most favored choice is always to shut up! And that was so evident in my *happy yellow* with a *dash of blue* personality! To understand that analogy, I highly recommend you read the Taylor Hartman

"Color Code" book and take the test, which you can also find online.

It will help you to understand yourself and others better. Very often, the hurt we experience in relationships is nothing more than just a misunderstanding and misinterpretation of the actions and words of others. I want to make myself clear on what I am not saying. No test is 100% accurate as the writer of the book states, the Color Code test is not intended to put anyone in a box. Every personality reflects a part of God's nature to the world. Each individual's unique personality is a gift from God to be a blessing, as Psalm 139:14 says we are fearfully and wonderfully made.

No temperament is better than or inferior to another. All are beautifully displayed through the life and ministry of Jesus Christ. He is red, the bold and courageous Lion of the tribe of Judah. He is blue, the relational and caring Shepherd. He is white, the gentle, meek Lamb of God that takes away the sins of the world, and He is yellow, the dancing, laughing, joyful God who sings over us.

Every human being is fashioned in the image of God, knit together in the secret place of their mother's womb. But because we are born into a fallen world, our image is marred by the sin of iniquity. We all have been wounded by words and deeds that impact our personality either for good or for evil. I wrote more about this in my book, "He Cares for Me."

As a new believer in the faith, when I read in Acts 8 that Christ was silent in His suffering, I used to take that as confirmation, I was to keep my mouth shut. I would never rock the boat, always keep the peace, and, if must be, let them slaughter me so that God would be glorified. Maybe you too have had that mindset, Acts 8:32 *"He was led as a sheep to the slaughter; And as a lamb before its shearer is silent, So He opened not His mouth..."*

My lens of a passive temperament, go along to get along, seemed to be, supported by this verse. That was because, as a new believer, I did not know how to divide the truth rightly. Thank God He doesn't leave as He finds us. If I kept my mouth shut, how could I ever be used by God to warn others of the impending danger of eternal separation from God? Isaiah 40:3-5 *The voice of one crying in the wilderness: "Prepare the way of the Lord; Make straight in the desert A highway for our God. 4 Every valley shall be exalted and every mountain and hill brought low; The crooked places shall be made straight and the rough places smooth; 5 The glory of the Lord shall be revealed, and all flesh shall see it together; For the mouth of the Lord has spoken."*

Many have referred to me as a life application teacher because I love to apply Scripture in a personal and practical way, as I demonstrate below with the verses you just read in Isaiah 40.

- He cries out loud interceding for me in my wilderness as He blazes a trail through the desert, just to find me.

- He turns the path before me into a superhighway, one that others can follow as well.

- He fills in the low places, every deficit with His love, and lifts me upon His shoulders.

- He blows up the high places that blocked my view of Him and level them flat like a pancake.

- He straightens out the crooked, twisted ways of thinking in my soul so I can walk upright.

- He gently buffs out the rough, sharp places and makes them smooth,

- So that His beautiful character, joyful nature, powerful peace, and His mighty strength can be seen through His very own daughter, me! And everybody going to see it because my Papa said so!

God used 'The American Renewal Project' as part of my training. They are the organization behind the massive statewide Governor prayer gatherings known as 'The Response.' They also offer free, all-expenses-paid, 'Issachar Training' to pastors and church leaders who attend 'The Response'. Their Biblical training teaches the mandate, that Christian leaders are called to serve in all seven mountains of culture, which are religion, family, education, government, media, arts and entertainment, and business. The name of the training comes from I Chronicles 12:32, *the sons of Issachar who understood the times, to know what Israel ought to do.*

The speakers were humble, dynamic, powerful, shakers and movers who were living out the mandate the Bible teaches to lead, not 'just in the church,' but in their city, state, and nation. I was blessed to attend two Issachar Trainings, as well as three of the five Response Prayer Gatherings which were held in;

- Houston, TX- Governor Rick Perry- August 2011

- Baton Rouge, Louisiana-Governor Bobby Jindal-January 2015

- Charleston, South Carolina-Governor Nikki Haley-June 2015

For two of the prayer gatherings, I had the joy of serving alongside the phenomenal Somebody Cares America team, from Houston, TX. Doug and his staff were the ones responsible for the logistics, all the administration, training the prayer candidates, and facilitating the entire event. Doug was the Master of Ceremony for all five Response prayer gatherings.

Following the Louisiana Response, we were all invited to the Governor's mansion for dinner. I thank the Lord for making room for me at His table and for Doug's relationships that made room for me at the Governor's mansion table. I am more than blessed, grateful, and humbled to have been a part of those historic gatherings praying for our nation.

After returning while giving a testimony of how the Lord moved at the Louisianan Response, a woman asked me, "How did you get invited to participate in the prayer gathering and invited to Governor Jindal's mansion for dinner?" I told her, "The Kingdom of God is built on relationships. Who, how, and where we serve will bring us before people and to places we would never have believed if told us.

It was the Biblical truth I learned from the 'Issachar Training' that prepared me for my next assignment from the Lord. When I received a call from the "Alliance Defense for Freedom,' I knew the training was for such a time as this! ADF is a lawyer defense organization defending the rights of Christians. I had the opportunity as one of four churches to sue the Attorney General of Massachusetts, in a court case of the violation of the First

Amendment. I never dreamed I would have an opportunity to testify of my faith by standing up for my freedom of speech to preach the Word of God.

The Legislators of Massachusetts passed legislation known as "the Bathroom Bill." They did so without allowing the people of Massachusetts to vote on the bill. The law stated that persons of any sexual orientation could use any bathroom in any public place, which identified churches among public places.

The bill stated that, based on the sexual preference a person identified with, not based on the gender they were born with, the law permitted use of any bathroom they preferred. This law put in danger any pastor preaching the religious ideal of marriage. It would be discriminating against those who chose to marry their same gender. The pastor would then be in violation of the law and would be fined $50,000.00 and serve up to one year in prison for each violation of the law. In other words, even though the Bible states; He made them male and female, a pastor is not allowed to discriminate anyone by calling someone a male or female if they don't see themselves as that gender.

At the time of this mess, Somebody Cares New England, for years had proven we were loving, honoring, and serving all people. We have never discriminated against anyone or tried to force Christianity on those we serve. Every human being deserves respect and dignity regardless of social, economic status, orientation, age, religion, or race. We are all made in the image of God, even if sinful ideologies and lifestyles may mar the individual's image.

In preparation for the court case, several of the lawyers were on a conference call coaching the four pastors preparing for the day in court. The Alliance Defense for Freedom gave the guidance needed for the Massachusetts pastors to file suit. We were not suing the state for their efforts to protect the LBGT community, every human life should be protected from harm. We were suing the State of Massachusetts for a violation of the first amendment. The issue was that houses of worship were not permitted by law to preach according to Scripture, that God's design for marriage is one man, one woman, which would force pastors to make the bathrooms in the house of worship unisex.

Several years prior, when all the hearings with the LGBT community began with Massachusetts legislators, many of us would go to the State House and quietly pray during these heated and intense sessions. During one of the breaks while in the ladies' room, I glanced at the size 15 shoe, (my guess), that a larger than life man was in the stall next to me. I felt instant panic and was horrified. I ran to the sink, quickly wash my hands when in the mirror, I could see behind me, out came this huge man, dressed like a woman with a blonde wig and hot pink lipstick, placing his hands under the same faucet as mine while looking in the mirror, snickering in my face.

I could not believe this was happening to me, in the State House, right in my face. I quickly ran out to find the policeman standing guard by the bathroom door. I frantically said, "Officer there is a man in the ladies' bathroom!" He looked at me with a blank stare for a brief moment as he motioned for me to keep moving and said, "Move along little lady, we don't need any trouble here." Any trouble? I am the one troubled, does that even matter?

During the ADF coaching phone call, the lawyer asked each of the four pastors to give to our interpretation of the 'Bathroom Bill' to make sure we had a proper understanding. When I finished giving my statement, one of the lawyers asked me, "Are you a lawyer?" I laughed out loud, "Not hardly, but I did attend 'Issachar Training,' which prepares pastors to be a proactive voice in the seven mountains of culture."

Their response was, "Well you certainly have a good understanding of the law. Our role is to present that side in the courtroom. We need you to speak on behalf of the church as a pastor." I quietly replied, "Got it, lets' try this again!" The second round when I finished, they all agreed I was a right fit for the task. They warned us all that we could be blackballed and targeted by the LGBT community, by government officials and identified on a local and national level as 'troublemakers.' The good news is, the AG's office settled out of court. They removed the language that included churches as a public place. The separation of church and state-protected the church as was intended!

Unfortunately, the 'Bathroom Bill' did pass, the people of the gay state, I mean the Bay State, led the nation again, as forerunners in their antichrist, anti-God movement by voting 'yes' on the November 2018 ballot. There are other ways to protect people from discrimination without violating the right of privacy for others. The times we are living have been foretold, there will be no surprises for those who know the Scriptures warning us of the last days. The question to the church is, "Are you willing to be the donkey warning of impending danger, or will the church be the 'little lady' told by the police officer, to be quiet?"

I am grateful to the Lord for the opportunity to *"hee-haw'*. Once I have warned, the outcome is none of my business, it's His. But be assured, there will come a day when the church will give an account for how we upheld the truth of the Word of God.

The 700 Club did a documentary on this mess titled, 'Massachusetts Pastors Challenge State Antidiscrimination Law," https://www.youtube.com/watch?v=W9qRbvpaI7Y 4:37. At the end of the documentary, the reporter asked me a question, "Are you aware that by not complying with the law, you could face charges, paying $50,000.00 in fines and up to a year in prison?" My answer to her, very calmly and peacefully, was, "I'd have a new ministry, in a new location, I have no fear."

What has God done with this little *'yellow with a dash of blue'* lady, who wouldn't just move along and be quiet? Could this be the evidence of transformation? Was that really me? A courageous *'red' donkey with a dash of peaceful 'white'* that carries His truth up the mountain of government. He was transforming the donkey to be a carrier of His presence into my Judea (capital), color code talk, you will love the book!

It didn't take long before the backlash predicted happened. I was now labeled a 'trouble maker.' Just because I was willing, as a pastor, to be a voice on the mountain of government, I heard from California and Florida, as well as local Christians, even those in my church weighed in.

Still today, the accusers can be heard with these recurring words, "Pastors like you are the reason that people hate God and the church." I thank the Lord for the opportunity to stand, like David, for righteousness with a heart of fearless humility in the face of the secular humanist giants in the land; I Samuel 17:28-29... *and Eliab's anger was aroused against David, and he said, "Why did you come down here? And with whom have you left those few sheep in the wilderness? I know your pride and the insolence of your heart, for you have come down to see the battle." 29 And David said, "What have I done now? Is there not a cause?"* It was David's brothers that accused him of pride and insolence (bold, rude, disrespectful, and insulting behavior). Although the accuser tried to use the "Bathroom Bill" challenge unfavorably, that does not mean the Lord does not favor me! As they say in France, au contraire! Remember, it was God who said, "Have you considered my servant Job?"

Most of the time, it is because of the favor of the Lord that we are lead into a conflict, not away from it. I received confirmation as I felt the pleasure of the Lord when reading this prayer, taken from one of my devotions during those days.

O God, nothing of earth's treasures shall seem dear to me if only You are glorified in my life. Be exalted over my friendships. I am determined that You are above all, though I must stand deserted and alone in the midst of the earth. Be exalted above my comforts. Though it means the loss of physical comforts and that I carry a heavy cross, I shall keep my vow made this day before You. Be exalted over my reputation. Make me ambitious to please You, even if as a result I must sink into obscurity and my name be forgotten as a dream. Rise, O Lord, into Your proper place of honor, above my ambitions, above my likes and dislikes, above family, my health and even my life itself. Let me decrease that You may increase; let me sink that You may rise above. Ride forth upon me as You did ride into Jerusalem mounted upon the humble little beast, a colt, the foal of an ass, and let me hear the children cry to Thee, "Hosanna in the highest." Matthew 21:5-11 A.W. Tozer The Pursuit of God, 101-102

Chapter 11

The Donkey and the Well

In chapter three, I wrote about the prayer assignment the Lord gave us to re-dig the wells of revival on the Northpoint Bible College campus (formerly Bradford College). It reminds me of the story of Jacob in Genesis 26:3-4, 18 *"Dwell in this land, and I will be with you and bless you; for to you and your descendants I give all these lands, and I will perform the oath which I swore to Abraham your father. 4 And I will make your descendants multiply as the stars of heaven; I will give to your descendants all these lands; and in your seed all the nations of the earth shall be blessed; 18And Isaac dug again the wells of water which they had dug in the days of Abraham his father, for the Philistines had stopped them up after the death of Abraham..."*

In 1999 when we bought our new home in Kingston, NH, it was during the first month of construction when I got to see them dig our well. It was not with the sweat of a man's back with a shovel in hand. It was with a man sitting behind the controls of a vast machine that did all the work.

I can only imagine the gruesome labor it must have been for those living in Biblical times to dig a well. Genesis 26 tells us the story about Jacob re-digging the wells his grandfather Abraham had dug for future generations. The enemy has no new tricks. He is always looking to fill the wells with dirt to prevent the next generation from having access to life-giving water for themselves, their little ones, and livestock.

Such was the case with Bradford Academy. Established in 1803, the initial vision of Parson Allen and thirty members of his congregation. They set out to dig a well of living water for their daughters to have a Christian education, preparing them for missions and marriage to pastors for church planting.

It was in 1932, under the leadership Dr. Karen Denworth, that the school began the transition from its original vision of Christian missions school into a liberal arts junior college for women. They focused on creative arts and social sciences as a category of academic disciplines (which is concerned with society and the relationships among individuals within a society). It later became a co-ed college in 1971. Bradford College, a liberal arts institution, replaced the former Bradford Academy campus and operated for 197 years. They had students from all over the world who came for their education. Then in 2000, due to a decline in student enrollment, enormous financial debt, and other reasons, they closed the campus—the wells of revival that our forefathers labored to dig on this property now filled with dirt.

The mantle dropped, the water supply cut off, but our Heavenly Father did not forget the covenant our forefathers made with Him.

It had been five years since Dr. Stringer prophesied that God wanted us to re-dig the wells on the campus. During that time, we had many conversations with believers from across New England. Their hearts shared in God's dream to re-dig the wells and reissue the call to missions. We met intercessors from across the nation as well that had been praying for the restoration of the mission sending movement long before we started our prayer journey in 2002.

There are many testimonies from the people that prayed during those years; one, in particular, is my favorite. A grandmother drove down to Haverhill from Dover, N. H., with her eight-year-old granddaughter to pray. Neither of them knew the original mission of the campus.

Friends only told them there was an abandoned property that they were claiming for the Kingdom of God.

When they got out of the car, her granddaughter started to shake and prophecy, "Nana, Nana, I see students coming from all over the world to this campus sent out as missionaries!" Isn't that just like the Lord to prophesy through a little one on behalf of their generation!

It was January 2007 when I met my dear friend Karen Chitty-Boe. She was a 1978 graduate of Zion Bible College in Rhode Island. I shared with her of the abandoned campus, and the local newspaper story written about the potential purchase of the former Bradford College property by Zion. She told me the college had run into a brick wall and had taken their offer off the table. We had a lively discussion about the perfect match of Zion's mission and the original purpose of the school. We were more than thrilled and both agreed, "This is the will of God for Zion, let's keep praying and watch God perform miracles."

At that moment, I remembered the word of the Lord over my life in 2004, "Step aside, daughter, I have a bulldozer, and I am going to breakthrough," and breakthrough He did! To tell the details of that story needs a book of its own, and there is one! Dr. Patrick G. Gallagher and Rosalie M. LoPinto wrote "A Journey of Faith," the inspiring story of Northpoint Bible College (formerly Zion Bible College).

In May 2007, just after Zion purchased the property, I had lunch with Karen, Dr. Gallagher, who was at the time Academic Dean of Students, and several others from the college. I was overly excited to meet him and offered to mobilize volunteers to assist with cleaning, painting, or anything else needed. He politely said, "Thank you." I had that a familiar feeling, I would often get, that he may have thought me to be a bit too over the top. I suspected the offer wasn't received.

I have a reputation for being a tad zealous; it is a defect; I mean characteristic of the yellow personality temperament. On more than one occasion, I have made a mess of things, proving that zeal without wisdom can be a problem. I have contemplated designing a tee-shirt with the words, "caution subject to outbursts of enthusiasm."

Many times, I have asked the Lord to tone me down. But what I have come to appreciate is that my yellow temperament is a gift and has a purpose. By His grace, I can see now in my later years; God did not change the divine design of my temperament. What He did was heal the brokenness in my soul and add His wisdom to the enthusiasm, thank God!

Dean Gallagher didn't know me from Adam, and I never gave him a chance to before I lunged at him with my enthusiastic offer. I was violating a fundamental relational principle found in Scripture, that I practice myself, which is, to know those who labor among you.

When the school transitioned from Rhode Island to Haverhill, the whole city did a happy dance! At that time Somebody Cares New England produced our own local cable TV show. I was thrilled the President of Zion (at that time), Dr. Crabtree, accepted my invitation as my guest on the show. He said something that day I will never forget, "We were praying in Rhode Island, Lord where do You want us to go?" You folks were here walking the campus all those years and praying, "Lord send a Bible College to this campus to re-dig the wells of revival and send missionaries out to the four corners of the earth again." "Well my sister, our prayers were heard in heaven. The Lord married our prayers and look at what He has done! Dr. Crabtree went on to say, "What He has done for us, God will do for you because He is the miracle-working God."

The school moved to Haverhill just in time for fall students to arrive. Several months later, while talking to the Lord, I asked, "Why? Why did I get to be a part of praying Your heart for this campus, but I don't get to serving, as was my hope to do?" I had so looked forward to serving. I love how the Holy Spirit interrupts our one-sided conversation as we are venting to Him. To my grateful surprise the Lord answered me from His Word; Ecclesiastes 9: 14-15 *"There was a little city with few men in it; and a great king came against it, besieged it, and built great snares around it. 15 Now there was found in it a poor wise man, and he by his wisdom delivered the city. Yet no one remembered that same poor man."*

I felt the Lord speak clearly to my heart through this verse, "I sent you on assignment, and you did well. Are you going to be ok if no one even remembers who you are and that I get the glory?" My humble response was, "Yes Sir, please forgive me. Thank you for allowing me to pray what Your heart for the campus was. It is enough for me, and I give You all the glory."

As years passed, more and more Northpoint students stumbled across the Somebody Cares New England (SCNE) outreach center. The center consisted of four storefronts. One was the church, which also served as the house of prayer, the Café where we served the homeless, a food pantry, storage, and Sunday school classes.

The Street Team of Northpoint loved the organic street ministry they experienced with our team. They started to bring back God sighting stories to the college of how the Lord was using the center as a refuge for the people on the streets. Students began to ask if they could do their internship with our church, CCF, and the SCNE outreach center. Go figure, after laying down my desire to serve the school; I was now serving the school through the students!

Isn't that just like the Lord? He lets us be a part of what He is doing, He then asks for us to give our part back to Him as an offering. It is only then He can trust us to give it back us; not the way we thought, but even better! He wants us to understand, just like a mother's womb is the secret place He fashions human life, it is a holy place where the Giver of life does His handiwork.

Intercession happens in the holy place, whereby in the fullness of time, the purposes of God come forth. Once that baby (ministry, church, etc.) is born, like Mary and Hannah, we dedicate that child back to God. That which is created belongs to the Creator. We are just the vessel, the carrier, the special place where He has chosen to procreate the human race, so it is with intercession.

I love how my friend Alan Bailey says it best, "God rented space in Mary's womb for the Savior to be born." God rented (borrowed) a dwelling space in my heart to pray His redemptive purpose for the campus. God knows our human inclination is to hold onto what He births through us. He must establish that he owns the rights to life and the rights to miracles; otherwise, we will rob Him of His glory.

Once we get it straight, He can trust us, just like the story in Genesis 21 of Abraham offering his son Isaac to God. Therein is the divine process; He uses us as His vessel to bring forth His promise. We lay down the promise on the altar of sacrifice, giving the promise back to God, then He gives us the promise back for us to steward. It reminds us we do not own the promise; we are only a steward of the promise. The definition steward: "a person who manages another's property or financial affairs; one who administers as the agent of another." We can do nothing in and of our selves. I need reminding over and over, it all belongs to Him, and He gets all the glory!

Fast forward years later, May 2018, there was a tragedy in our city, right on the corner of our building. A young man was shot and killed in a gang-related incident. The corner block was the focus of police, news reporters, and hundreds of young people that set up a memorial of liquor bottles, stuffed animals, poetry, and candles that burned 24 hours for weeks, just four feet from our front steps.

The Mayor frequented my office during those weeks. On one occasion, he said, "Marlene I need you to start a youth center here on the hill for the youth. There is nothing for them up on 'the hill' and they need help. As Mayor of this city, I want you to know, we would be willing to help you do it."

For twenty years, we have been reaching out to the youth of our city, as well as other cities. But now we were talking something much different than an outreach. We knew this was an invitation from God; it was time for a sustained presence for the young people.

The leaders took the request; we knew this would be a huge undertaking. It was going to require many changes. We bore witness to the plea that came through our Mayor and diligently sought the Lord for His wisdom to do it.

For six months, we prayed, strategized, planned, and prepared. At that time, we thought we needed to find a second campus for our church to move the daily church activities to another location. We knew we needed to make room for the growing demands the youth center was going to bring. We started to cast the vision and search out a second campus. The second location would be in addition to the Sunday church service we were currently having. We knew the SCNE food pantry was the perfect way to introduce the youth center. We are grateful for CCF Ministries of Haverhill, who own the building giving SCNE space to use as our outreach center. We have seen how the Lord has used the two ministries to build a relational bridge to the families on 'the hill.'

One day while looking out the office window, I saw, as if for the first time, the street signs Washington St and Shepherd St. together on the corner. The revelation came that we were planted strategically on 'the hill' with both (Washington) natural and (Shepherd) spiritual governmental authority. We now have a greater understanding; it is for such a time as this, we were sent to the hill by God's divine design. It was soon after that revelation we invited the prophetic movement team from Pastors Eliot and Evelyn Penn's New Life Church in Chelsea, Massachusetts. They came and ministered for our Sunday morning service. One of the prophetic movement dances was to the song, "The Hill" by Travis Greene.

Sin around me

Pain is in me

Stress is on me

But I gotta keep looking up

Tears are streaming

Heart is beating

Others leaving

But I gotta keep looking up

Some will trust in horses and chariots

But I will look to the hills, and I will not fear

Some may say that they found another way

But my eyes are on you, and I will not move from the hill.

During this song, I had an epiphany, and my heart exploded with joyful tears streaming down my face. God sent us to 'the hill' with the backing of heaven, to stake out territory under the banner of the cross of Christ. Sent to decree and declare the power of His shed blood to save, heal, and deliver a people who would come to know Him.

When we hear His voice of authority speaking to our hearts it is time to take notice, stand up saying, "Yes, Sir!" speak through Your servant, and I will lift my voice like a trumpet.

> Isaiah 40:9 *O Zion, you who bring good tidings, get up into the high mountain; O Jerusalem, You who bring good tidings, Lift up your voice with strength, Lift it up, be not afraid; Say to the cities of Judah, "Behold your God*

> Revelation 1:10 *I was in the Spirit on the Lord's day, and I heard behind me a loud voice like the sound of a trumpet.*

I leave you with this humorous Jewish fable. One day a farmer's donkey fell down a well. The animal cried piteously for hours as the farmer worked hard, trying to get it out. Finally, he decided the animal was old and as the well needed to be covered up. It just wasn't worth trying to retrieve the donkey.

He asked all his neighbors to come and help him. They all brought a shovel and began shoveling dirt into the well. The donkey, of course, realized what was going on and began to bellow loudly, but after a while, suddenly went quiet.

After a few more shovelfuls, the farmer had to have a look and see why the donkey was quiet. To his amazement, as each shovelful fell onto the donkey, it just shook it off and then stepped onto it. As the farmer and his neighbors continued to shovel dirt into the well, the donkey just kept shaking it off and stepping up. Pretty soon, the donkey reached the top of the well, climbed out, and trotted away quite happily.

The moral of this story? Life is going to shovel dirt on you, the key to getting out of the well is to shake it off and stomp on it, put it under our feet. We can get out of the deepest wells just by not stopping and never giving up. So, shake it off, step it up!

This fable reminds me of the children of Israel, as mentioned in Genesis 26. How many times had their enemies filled up the wells with dirt to stop their access to water? This act of filling wells with dirt was commonly regarded as legitimate ancient warfare. It was an act to cut off Isaac, making it impossible for his flocks and herds to exist without access to water supplies. It was probably, as the text indicates, the outcome of envy. In re-digging and possessing wells, Isaac was re-claiming ownership of the land.

Halleluiah! The breakthrough comes after the warfare has ended. When the world sees the whites of the donkey's eyes (the carriers of His presence, the church) rising out of the dirt, they will see the Kingdom of God indeed, not just in word! Then they will come to drink from the wells of revival and enjoy the fruit of our labors!

It was for such a time as this. He confirmed to us that half of the team would serve on 'the hill' location and the other half on the new location for the CCF Ministries church plant DBA 'Renaissance City Church.' We all agreed that our new assignment was to reach college and career age, entrepreneurs, and the renaissance (artist) population in our city. We are the first-ever in the history of our city to be a church planting explicitly targeting this population.

If you remember, in an earlier chapter, the Mayor said, "Haverhill Massachusetts is a renaissance city in transformation." God used our Mayor to inspire the name of our new church plant, Renaissance City Church. Our leadership staff spied the land looking for the location for this new work. After months of dead ends, we threw our hands in the air (in praise). We knew our efforts were not going to make this thing happen, all the while casting the vision and thanking Him for leading us into the promised land.

Then one glorious moment, it happened! Pastor Dave Hanshumaker called me ecstatic, "What about Northpoint Bible College auditorium for the new church?" Of course, my response was very yellow! "YIKES, could this be the open door as spoken by Dr, Bigpond, "It's time to cross the river?" After all, Northpoint is located across the river from CCF. Pastor Dave and his wife Pastor Donna are graduates of Northpoint and worked there on staff for many years. Dave met with President Arnett to share the vision. It was a perfect match for the school and the new church plant. We hoped to serve the college, and we now 'get to' do it while serving our city together!

Dr. Arnett desired for the school to train their students in the arts for the preaching of the Gospel; so, of course, the All-Wise, All-

Knowing God moved Alan and Kate Bailey to Haverhill as missionaries to do just that! Alan had served as Professor of Music for Northpoint for many years. He left to take a position as a worship director at a church in Arizona.

While serving in Arizona, God spoke to both he and his wife. The Lord told them to move back to Haverhill and serve with Marlene Yeo as missionaries to the city. Alan is a graduate of the New England Conservatory of Music and a gifted musician, song, and play writer! He and Kate served as Director of Creative and Performing Arts for our church. They are a perfect fit sent out with the Pastoral staff with lead pastors Dave and Donna at "Renaissance City Church."

One of the things I always asked the Lord for is lasting fruit as evidence that my life and my labor in the Lord would not in vain. I am not a blow in, blow up and blow out kind of girl. Although that is a characteristic of yellow temperaments, the Lord has worked His red like strength in my personality. I am now a dig in the heals, come hell or high water, die in my boots with a sword in my hand, kind of girl! I have fought the good fight and choosing daily to finish the race well. I thank God that I get to live out my later years serving the leaders on the hill and across the river! CCF Ministries is one church, many locations!

You can't make this stuff up. Only God, Master weaver, networker, builder, and miracle worker made a way for Northpoint to come to Haverhill. He restored the campus, re-fired the call of missions, and made room for those who labored in prayer to have a place to minister on that same property! Indeed, the city of God is a renaissance city in transformation!

It is a joy to partner with the Lord and Northpoint Bible College in facilitating the Tower of Prayer on the campus in the mini chapel every Sunday night from 6:30-8:00 pm. We invite believers across the Valley to intercede for revival fire to sweep our land as we pray the model of the Moravian prayer movement. To better understand the prayer transformation model for the Tower of Prayer view:

- The Moravian Prayer movement (sound bite version) 5:01

https://www.youtube.com/watch?v=xRs9YkCvM_8

- For more of the story 1:06:35 Moravian Mission Machine

https://www.youtube.com/watch?v=eQNWCQbm4bc

The prayer culture of intercession in the Tower of Prayer is worship and praying the promises of God in the wisdom and power of the Holy Spirit. We do not speak to God about the culture (He already knows what is in our culture), we speak over the culture God's Word, and call those things that are not as though they were. We rule over the principalities by coming in faith, decreeing, and declaring the will of God. It is a corporate prayer gathering, where we lift our voice like a trumpet and blow the trumpet preparing the way of the Lord.

Chapter 12

Is That a Donkey or a Horse?

For many years Margret (Peggy) Foley and I kept the Drop-in Center open on Monday Holidays. Before given the key to open the center, people from the shelter wandered the streets every holiday. The center is the only place the homeless, alcoholics, addicts, and the mentally ill can go during the day for food, shelter, and services. When we first started on Monday holidays, Bill, the Director, would drop by mid-morning to check on us. He always looked a bit worried that us little ladies would not know what to do if a situation arose, that is until this one day.

While I was sitting at the desk, Bill walked over to let me know he was leaving. The very thing he was worried might happen, happened. He got to see how this little donkey handles a not so pleasant situation. There was a list of policies and procedures set by the Director of the center on every wall. The process of phone usage was to sign up; and wait for their turn. As I was looking at the list to call the next person, this massive, pungent, filthy man, neither Bill nor I had ever seen before, approached the desk and using profanity, demanding to use the phone. I calmly and politely answered, "I am happy to add you to the list and call you when it is your turn; what is your name?"

That did not go well with him. He torqued it up, going off on a tangent. For mine and the sake of others, I had to stop his flood of filthy, vile, aggressive speech. Talking over him, I firmly said, "I am treating you with respect, and I would appreciate you to do likewise. You will not be permitted to talk to anyone here like that."

Yah, that didn't help either. I could not believe the things he was saying. It was straight from the bowels of hell. I stood to my feet, looked him square in the eyes, and said, "In the name of Jesus Christ, I command you to shut up and leave now!"

He started to walk backward toward the door. I kept eye contact with him as he went. Elaine, one of the volunteers with our ministry was pouring coffee, as he passed by her, he leaned over to say something. I jumped up, pointed at the door, and told him to get out and not to say another word. I was not about to let a demonically oppressed man torment a volunteer or intimidate me, especially with the director of the center sitting right there.

A couple of the homeless guys were outside smoking, hearing the commotion, they came running in saying, "We'll take care of him for you, pastor Yeo." The whole time I continued to look the man in straight in the eyes while saying, "No need guys, he's leaving, everything's ok." I followed him out the door as he walked down the sidewalk, muttering and sputtering under his breath. I stood there to make sure he was not returning anytime soon. Suddenly, he turns, glaring at me with a look of rage and screams at me, "YOU...YOU HORSE!

I thought to myself, horse? A horse of all things to call me, I don't even have a ponytail! It made no sense, and I found it quite hilarious. I thought to myself, is that all you got? We went back inside, Bill looking at me wide-eyed with his mouth open, said, "Well, I guess I don't need to worry about you handling things around here. He paused and then said, "I am trying to wrap my mind around what just happened." It was yet another opportunity to witness to Bill about the power of the Name of Jesus.

I told him, "We show love and respect to all people, but we don't tolerate abuse. I had tried to reason with the man politely. When that didn't work, I had to use my spiritual authority in Christ because you can't reason with a demon, you have to command it."

Later that day, when I got home, I was thinking about the crazy incident. Laughing out loud, I said to the Lord, "A demon called me a horse, that is hilarious; I would not have been surprised if that spirit called me the backside of a donkey but a horse?

That may have bothered you that I said it was a demon that called me a horse. The gift of discerning of spirits has on occasion separated believers from fellowship with one another. I've had several lively conversations with Christians regarding the gifts of the Spirit. Discerning of spirits is another gift many have difficulty accepting. Believers can be influenced by demonic ideology regarding discernment. They may not have read that Jesus rebuked, even His disciples. It was to Peter He said, "Get thee behind me, Satan." And in Luke 9:55, Jesus rebuked the disciples because they wanted to call down fire on the city of

Samaria, saying to them, "You do not know what manner of spirit you are of."

Maybe the believers I've had conversations with haven't had the exciting opportunity to experience the need for the discerning of spirits. Or perhaps they are influenced by a deceiving spirit themselves. Either way, I gingerly end the awkward conversation by saying, "We can agree to disagree."

Sometimes it is wise not to tip over that 'unholy cow.' There have even been some that left our church because of this very thing. I don't take it personal or get offended. You cannot give someone else your revelation of truth or your experience, that is the Holy Spirit's job. I just bless them as they mysteriously disappear and pray for them to have a personal encounter that will reveal their need for understanding the gift of discerning of spirits.

In searching the Bible and using several study tools, looking for answers, I found that biblical symbolism of a horse has significance. During the Middle Ages, virgin heroes and saints rode upon a white horse. At the end of the age, Christ and His heavenly armies arrive, mounted on white horses (Rev 19:11-15). The horse means power, strength, courage, conquest and spiritual warfare. One commentary said a white horse is a symbol of revival. In biblical times horses were the property of kings and not of the ordinary people.

I sincerely believe the spirit that was speaking through the demonized man that called me a horse recognized Christ's authority in me. I am grateful for the opportunity I had that day. I saw the evidence of what the Holy Spirit's power had done in me. I was no longer the timid, frightened, insecure believer He rescued when He saved me. He is transforming me into a strong, courageous, warrior bride. I especially loved; a horse was the property of kings and not ordinary people. YES! I am no longer the property of, owned or possessed by the fear of man. I belong to the King!

Scripture tells us the devil not only discerned but also announced publically who the Lord was, as well as recognizing His disciples.

> Luke 8:28 *When he saw Jesus, he cried out, fell down before Him, and with a loud voice said, "What have I to do with You, Jesus, Son of the Most High God? And Acts 16:16-18 Now it happened, as we went to prayer, that a certain slave girl possessed with a spirit of divination met us, who brought her masters much profit by fortune-telling. 17 This girl followed Paul and us, and cried out, saying, "These men are the servants of the Most High God, who proclaim to us the way of salvation." 18 And this she did for many days. But Paul, greatly annoyed, turned and said to the spirit, "I command you in the name of Jesus Christ to come out of her." And he came out that very hour.*

On another day at the Drop-in Center, a mentally ill woman I had never met before came to the desk to sign in and promptly said to me, "Whoa! Kathryn Kulman is here with the healing power of God in her hands." I am sure the expression on my face revealed I was unsure of how to answer; I never want to carry on a conversation with a demon. I smiled, thinking to myself, what is going on right now? Just then, my daughter Bethany walked through the door, and this same lady announces to the entire room, "Whoa, when you walked in, every demon took notice."

Although I think it amusing when this stuff happens, I take it as confirmation that the spirit realm sees more than most professing Christians do. I don't rejoice that the demons recognize the power of Christ in me; I rejoice that He wrote my name in the Lamb's book of life.

I learned years ago that the power of the Lord is my only defense, my strong tower where I find safety and refuge. The experiences that God has allowed to cross my path along this adventurous journey have never been intended for my harm, although the enemy meant it for evil. Instead, it has been my training to help rescue lives. Genesis 50:20 *But as for you, you meant evil against me; but God meant it for good, to bring it about as it is this day, to save many people alive.*

When in a hard place, sometimes we need to be reminded, it was the Spirit that led Jesus into the wilderness (Matthew 4:1). And Hosea writes, the wilderness is where He comforts and reveals more of who He is to us.

> Hosea 2:14-16 *"Therefore, behold, I will allure her, will bring her into the wilderness, and speak comfort to her. 15 I will give her, her vineyards from there, And the Valley of Achor as a door of hope; She shall sing there, as in the days of her youth, as in the day when she came up from the land of Egypt. 16 "And it shall be, in that day," says the Lord, "That you will call Me 'My Husband,' And no longer call Me 'My Master,'*

So, why all the talk about spiritual warfare? Why, if Christ defeated the enemy at the cross, stripping him of his power and authority, do we have to fight battles? Because when we do, we get to experience the victory that Christ won on Calvary! He will always cause us to triumph so that others see His power, which is our testimony and many are saved. The saving of souls is never because of us but because we partnered with the Resurrected Lord in His victory. Revelation 21:7 NIV *Those who are victorious will inherit all this, and I will be their God, and they will be my children.* Those who are victorious will inherit *all this*, that is, our inheritance and the new heaven and the new earth. We will rule and reign with Him according to how we ruled and reigned with Him while on the earth.

The Church of Jesus Christ will not leave this earth without a shout, a trumpet, and the final *big hullabaloo*! His return will be riding on a white horse, and He is coming for a pure, spotless Bride dressed in white. Romans 8:18-19 *For I consider that the sufferings of this present time are not worthy to be compared with the glory which shall be revealed in us. 19 For the earnest expectation of the creation eagerly waits for the revealing of the sons of God.*

The grievous moments of this present life will not compare to the coming glory promised. We may have entered our Jerusalem as a donkey, but we will enter the New Jerusalem riding on a white horse with none other the Lord Himself in the lead!

Revelation 19:11-16 *Now I saw heaven opened, and behold, a white horse. And He who sat on him was called Faithful and True, and in righteousness, He judges and makes war. 12 His eyes were like a flame of fire, and on His head were many crowns. He had a name written that no one knew except Himself. 13 He was clothed with a robe dipped in blood, and His name is called*

The Word of God. 14 And the armies in heaven, clothed in fine linen, white and clean, followed Him on white horses. 15 Now out of His mouth goes a sharp sword, that with it, He should strike the nations. And He Himself will rule them with a rod of iron. He Himself treads the winepress of the fierceness and wrath of Almighty God. 16 And He has on His robe and on His thigh a name written: KING OF KINGS AND LORD OF LORDS!

The Lord has taken off our grave clothes, arrayed us in battle clothes, and is sending us out, preparing the way for others to follow. It's time the world see the power, authority, and strength of the church clothed in humility, meekness, and love.

The challenge for us beloved is how we live out our faith amid the warfare. Let us not grow weary in well-doing; when the Master comes, may He find us full of faith and joy! I pray at the time of His soon return, we will be found doing Kingdom business. We will be faithful tending the vineyard, guarding the sheep, hands lifted in victory, singing the high praises of God with our mouth, and with a two-edged sword in our hand, preaching the gospel with signs and wonders following!

He is our Deliverer as written in Proverbs 21:31 *The horse is prepared for the day of battle, but deliverance is of the Lord.* We are those who stay pressed in seeking the Lord to sustain us while we find rest and refreshing in His presence, even as we fight the good fight. We do not need to be as those who grow weary running with the footman if we stay in the river of His love while we pray and look for His coming. Jeremiah 12:5 *"If you have run with the footmen, and they have wearied you, Then how can you contend with horses? And if in the land of peace, in which you trusted, they wearied you, Then how will you do in the floodplain of the Jordan?*

Old Testament prophecy declared that His first coming would be lowly and meek riding on a donkey (Zechariah 9). His second coming, the final conflict, the Lord of hosts will make Judah His royal warhorse and "HOLINESS TO THE LORD" will be engraved on the bells of the horses (Zechariah 14).

The title of this book is probably not one that would draw just anyone to read it, that is unless they have prayed, "Lord, I want to be a donkey for you!" Donkeys are disciples in training, learning obedience through suffering. They don't tell their Master where they will go or what they will do. They are willing to be carried by the Spirit, driven by the wind of God.

They will be known as a part of the *Fellowship of the Unashamed*. Being a Christian is an exciting, dangerous, and glorious life. The Spirit will take you to places beyond your control, out of your comfort zone, into unchartered waters, through seasons and experiences you would never choose. It takes strong, courageous faith to step out, let go, and let God use you to carry His presence into your Jerusalem.

I leave you with *The Charge*, supposed to have been written and circulated in conservative, evangelical circles in the late 1980s, said to have originated during the Bush War of the Rhodesia/Zimbabwe Conflict. The story told is that a young village pastor wrote this the night before his death. Despite all the research available on the internet today, the origin of this note cannot be verified. But, for me, it is a reminder of our call to be His disciple.

The Charge of the Fellowship of the Unashamed

I am a part of the *fellowship of the unashamed.*

I have Holy Ghost Spirit power.

The die has been cast. I have stepped over the line; the decision has been made. I am a disciple of His.

I won't look back, let up, slow down, back away, or be still.

My past is redeemed, my present makes sense, my future is secure.

I am finished and done with low living, cheap talking, sight walking, chintzy giving, dwarf goals, smooth knees, colorless dreams and tamed visions

I no longer need pre-eminence, prosperity, position, promotions, plaudits or popularity.

I don't have to be right, first, top, recognized, praised, regarded, or rewarded.

I know live by presence, lean by faith, walk with patience, lift by prayer and labor by power.

My face is set, my gait is fast, and my goal is heaven.

My road is narrow, my way is rough, my companions are few, and my guide reliable. My mission is clear. I cannot be bought, compromised, detoured, lured away, turned back, diluted or delayed.

I will not flinch in the face of sacrifice, hesitate in the presence of the adversary, negotiate with the enemy, ponder at the pool of popularity, or meander in the maze of mediocrity. I won't give up, let up, shut up until I have stayed up, stored up, prayed up, paid up, preached up for the cause of Christ. I am a disciple of Jesus. I must go until He comes, give until I drop, preach until all know, and work until He stops me. And when He comes for His me, He will have no problem recognizing me, for my colors will be clear!

About the Artist

Thank you, Martha Temple, my dear friend, and co-laborer for the beautiful paintings you did for this book. "The Donkey Descent into Jerusalem" for the cover and the last chapter painting, "Returning on a White Horse." Martha has been on the journey of city transformation with me since 1999. If you are interested in her painting she works by commission. To see more of her artwork, check out the Renaissance City Church Facebook page, or FB friend request her or email <u>zo3e7@comcast.net</u>

About the Author

Marlene J. Yeo is the founder, and executive director of Somebody Cares New England and founder and director of He Cares for Me, a ministry of healing and deliverance and pioneer of the Haverhill "Tower of Prayer." To find out more about her ministries, schedule her to speak or to purchase other books listed below, Facebook message: Marlene J. Yeo or email marlenejyeo@gmail.com

"Where is God on Tuesday" Read about her salvation and personal journey of deliverance, healing and wholeness and call to ministry.

"He Cares for Me" A book to equip the body of Christ for the ministry of healing and deliverance in the local church.

"He is Looking for a Donkey…to ride into your city," a book for prayer compassion missionaries who want to serve in intercession for transformation and revival.

Ministry websites:

www.ccfhaverhill.com

www.somebodycaresne.org

www.hecaresforme.org

www.renaissancecitychurch.org

CPSIA information can be obtained
at www.ICGtesting.com
Printed in the USA
JSHW031113290521
15242JS00001B/1